ROAD MOVIES

MARK WILLIAMS

DEDICATION

Dedicated to the memory of

JAMES ANGUS WOOD
21st. March 1946 – 27th. September 1981
Sadly missed by many, a good friend and inspiration to me,
and a man who appreciated a big V-8!

ROAD MOVIES

"With all their speed forward, they may be a step backward in civilisation. It may be that they won't add to the beauty of the world, of the life of men's souls. I'm not sure.

"But the automobile has come and almost all the outward things are going to be different because of what they bring. I think that men's minds are going to be changed in subtle ways because of automobiles.

"It may be that in ten or twenty years from now, if we can see the inward change in men by that time, I shouldn't be able to defend the gasoline engine, but I would have to agree that automobiles had no business being invented."

— Eugene Morgan, in THE MAGNIFICENT AMBERSONS

"I just wanna race motorcycles and screw people."

— Little Fauss, in LITTLE FAUSS & BIG HALSY

MARK WILLIAMS

PROTEUS BOOKS is an imprint of
The Proteus Publishing Group

United States
PROTEUS PUBLISHING CO., INC.
733 Third Avenue
New York, N.Y. 10017

distributed by:
THE SCRIBNER BOOK COMPANIES, INC.
597 Fifth Avenue
New York, N.Y. 10017

United Kingdom
PROTEUS (PUBLISHING) LIMITED
Bremar House,
Sale Place,
London, W2 1PT.

ISBN 0 86276 053 4 (p/b)
0 86276 054 2 (h/b)

Design	Rocking Russian
Editor	Nicky Hodge
Typeset	Wordsmiths of Street, Somerset, BA16 0LQ
Printed	Printer Industria Gráfica sa, Barcelona, Spain
DLB	29267 – 1982

ACKNOWLEDGEMENTS

I would like to express my appreciation to the librarians at the Academy of Motion Picture Arts & Sciences, Los Angeles, California, and the New York Public Library, Drama Department, Lincoln Center, for their forebearance and help during my lightning raids on their files. The same gratitude is offered to the ladies of the British Film Institute Library in London who, I'm glad to say, didn't have to put up with quite such a war of attrition.

Paul and Donna Gordon are due considerable thanks for housing me during a period of feverish research, as are Deborah Wood, Charlie Janson and Titi at Stansbatch Farm, who endured a similarly chaotic spell of typewriter activity.

Finally, there's Annabel Bartlett, who deserves a lot more than a brief acknowledgement, and I hope she knows why.

INTRODUCTION

"Wherever we're going, man, I'm *ready*!" yells Jeff Bridges, a big, dumb grin on his face as he jumps into Clint Eastwood's Oldsmobile. And in that one nanosecond of brattish glee, Michael Cimino's script for THUNDERBOLT & LIGHTFOOT said reams about being young, American and on the road.

I mean, there's something indefinably sensuous, sexy even, in the simple act of getting behind the wheel of a monstrous great car, experiencing a tingle of anticipation as the turn of a key unleashes muted thunder from a huge V-8, waiting for the choke to release its stranglehold on the carburettor and permit the steady throb of tick-over, gingerly snicking the shift-lever through 'R' and 'N' into 'D', and provoking a mean squeal from the rear tyres as you deliberately boot the gas.

Terrific! Suddenly you're on your way, across town or across America, fuelled by a gung-ho bravura that only a big car in a big country can bring out in a kid. It's you and your Chevvy against the world; a populist image every bit as real and inviolate as the Things That Go Better With Coke... or at least as long as petrol cost 35 cents a gallon and words like Datsun and Toyota remained outside the contemporary automobile argot.

All of which was a long time ago and, like much else that has since faded from the American dream, cheap fun with large cars has been engorged by Hollywood and turned into a highly commercial folk image. Behind the celluloid facade there is, however, a complex interplay of social mores involving the fondly-held notions and defeated expectations that characterise an American's relationship with his car. Some film-makers have attempted to address this by introducing heavy-handed allegorical devices of one sort or another, and some have concerned themselves with the ephemeral flotsam of car culture. Still others have directed their attentions to the curiosity value of less common transports of American delight; the truck and the motorcycle.

But for the most part, the cinema's treatment of mankind's strange and often passionate affair with the internal combustion engine is best exemplified by the "road movie".

Broadly speaking, there are two types of road movie; those that simply pander to car chauvinism, and those that exploit a nation's belief in the freedom that lies across a state line or two, with a car being the means to that end. (Rarely can a writer produce a script which embraces both of these elements successfully. Indeed it's a sorry comment on the state of the Hollywood literati, that the author of VANISHING POINT, probably the best of these dual-purpose rarities is a Spanish-Cuban living in England!). Having already established that a young American growing up in the 'fifties and 'sixties expected a huge, energy-squandering automobile as his God-given right, another, somewhat more reasonable assumption confronts those who would wish to understand the road movie phenomenon, and that is the innate restlessness of the American people.

I believe that it is this deeply ingrained desire to keep moving more than anything else that accounts for the endless catalogue of movies on wheels. America is, after all, a country with a comparatively short history. Only a couple of hundred years ago the first settlers were making the slow trek west, looking for somewhere to put down the roots they'd so painfully withdrawn in an economically depressed and politically troubled Europe. Those whose fortunes were tied up in cattle rather than in commerce or industry – and that was a lot of people – pushed their herds from pasture to pasture, a wanderlust prompted by the simple necessity of food. Then, as the land was subsequently wrested from the native Indians, or simply fenced off from the wild, agriculture created the property owning classes. And, as John Steinbeck sagely commented in 'Travels With Charley':

"...land is tangible, and tangibles have a way of getting into a few hands. Thus it was that one man wanted ownership of land and at the same time wanted servitude because someone had to work it. Roots were ownership of land, in tangible and immovable possessions. In this view we are a restless species with a very short history of roots, and those not widely distributed. Perhaps we have overrated roots as a psychic need. Maybe the greater the urge (for them), the deeper and more ancient is the need, the will, the hunger to be somewhere else."

It's a proposition Steinbeck has mined many times in his writing, and one that lies at the core of what's generally considered as being the earliest proper road movie, Darryl F. Zanuck's 1940 production of THE GRAPES OF WRATH. One important facet of John Ford's direction of GRAPES, is the pervasive feeling that, although the Joad family are forced by ill-luck and gnawing poverty to keep looking for the new deal that constantly eludes them, they are perhaps *driven* by a compulsion to remain mobile. In later films, this is expressed rather more simplistically as a love for the road itself.

To fully understand why this might be, you really have to spend some time travelling through the vast belly of middle America (an excruciating pun which nevertheless has relevance later on). The chic, cosmopolitan hinterlands of the seaboards, New York, Boston, Chicago, Los Angeles, San Francisco etc., are worlds apart from the slow, steady rhythms of the South, Mid-West and North-East. Although there are many large cities in these areas, their low-technology industries and haphazard urban sprawl confirms the rural antecedents of their citizenry. And as much as a Detroit foundryman would think little of driving twelve miles across town to sink a beer at his favourite bar, the farmers and small businessmen who live scattered throughout the vast agricultural belts are undaunted by the prospect of travelling seventy or eighty miles for dinner with friends.

In either case, the preferred conveyance is, of course, a large American sedan or coupé. Despite petrol prices that have quadrupled since the mid-1960s, old habits die hard and it's quite easy to see why. During those golden years, the cars that rolled out of the Motor City were designed with comfort primarily in mind. Veritable sitting-rooms on wheels, with low-stressed, effortlessly torqued six– and eight-cylinder engines and power-operated everything, they made bearable what were otherwise boring and bum-numbing journeys.

It's also a delicate but unavoidable truth that many Americans, fed on three big squares of meat'n'potatoes every day, are physically just too damn big to fit into a neat little Japanese or European econo-box. This, incidentally, is one of the reasons Detroit had difficulty in making the compromises between the traditional requirements of the home market, and the high-mileage threat from the Orient. Blaming the oil-sheiks was too easy – maybe they should have criticised the nation's eating habits instead.

Big country = big people = big cars. It's a circular equation wherein the solution is inevitably the problem. Thirty or forty years ago, however, the very bigness of America was most graphically realised in the form of the cowboy movie. But since the car replaced the horse as the prime mover, the road movie has all but superceded the western. All that remains intact is the wistful symbolism and the impressive natural backdrops which emphasise the scale and richness of the country.

In the western this huge, natural stage saw hackneyed themes of love, greed, friendship and revenge revitalised by picaresque characterisations, figures that were dramatically enhanced by the uncertainty and raw challenge of the pioneer era. The simple struggles of a disparate people trying to normalise life and scratch an income in a massive, hostile landscape was, in itself, often enough to carry such a film... or a television series. Road movies involve plots of a similar nature, the problems and choices are still made pretty plain, and the protagonist remains the common man trying to make it against easily identifiable odds.

Perhaps, as the director of DEATHRACE 2000 and CANNONBALL, Paul Bartel, contends, "The decline of the western just happened to coincide with the rise of the road movie. I'm not so sure that one was responsible for the other. There are two factors to bear in mind here. Firstly, we have in this country two generations of kids who've grown up without really knowing what public transportation can mean. Because the automobile industry is so important to the economy, other forms of transport have been short-changed, especially on the west coast, which is where all the films are made and which is where all the public funds have been put into building roads.

"Also, the U.S. film industry is completely audience motivated; the main reason for making films in this country is to satisfy an interest or demand on the part of audiences. I've explained why cars are second nature to kids here, and the fact of that mobility was responsible for cars becoming an expression of the independence of youth. The youth market has always been very important to Hollywood, and when that market demanded films that somehow commented on or reinforced their independence, movies about cars were the inevitable result.

"In American films, action is a very important ingredient too, and a car provides that beautifully... fast driving and lots of crashing!"

Returning to the demise of the western, Bartel continues: "There are fewer traces of the 'Old West' left nowadays, anyway. Even those old comics and books, the Zane Grey books, that kept the West alive, aren't being read anymore. In fact, with television and everything, kids generally read a lot less than they did, say, fifteen years ago. And so that avenue of access is closed."

Richard Sarafian, director of VANISHING POINT, believes the change to road movies was more tangible, and specifically related to cultural shifts. "I don't think that westerns satisfy today's audience because, although a guy riding round on a horse is perhaps vaguely recognised as part of America's heritage, it's too far removed from the times we're living in now. Kids can only look back so far and make the connections, and in today's media-intensive society, the world of their fathers' is about as far as they can manage. Cowboys and indians were no part of that, and people are looking for heroes and plots and themes in a form they're more familiar with. Certainly you could get into all kinds of complex values and relationships in westerns if you really wanted to, but the backgrounds are now terribly out-dated."

So the car, and to a lesser extent, the truck and the motorcycle, are the horse and stage coach of the new age. They are the means by which freedom is realised and honour upheld. The truckstop, burger-house, and gas station that cluster around every highway intersection have replaced the frontier town and trading post. But in terms of structure, the similarities are even more obvious. For example, the vehicle is an ever ready transport from one scene to another, and one with which an actor develops a bond as close as that which Roy Rogers felt for Trigger. Warren Oates' loud-mouthed pride for his Trans-Am in TWO LANE BLACKTOP, or Mark Hamill's puppy-love for his customised Corvette Stingray in CORVETTE SUMMER are just two other instances of this. And in THE GIRL ON A MOTORCYCLE Marianne Faithfull takes such sentiments to an extreme by having an orgasm every time she whacks open the throttle... which is maybe what we should expect from Marianne Faithfull and a motorcycle if the chauvinism of most road movie directors is to be admitted.

Women are usually depicted as weak, stupid or wretched in any film involved with vehicles and travelling. Upholding all the worst cliches about mandatory domesticity, road movies rarely feature a woman behind the wheel, unless she's making a fool of herself or her male companion's fallen asleep. Ali MacGraw in THE GETAWAY is the only exception that springs to mind, whilst we get a brief glimpse of Gilda Texter riding a Honda in VANISHING POINT, and a belligerent Karen Lamm brandishing a hammer at troublesome motorists as she rides her Yamaha through THUNDERBOLT AND LIGHTFOOT. Sometimes a female character is treated sympathetically, as with Goldie Hawn in SUGARLAND EXPRESS or Sondra Locke in THE GAUNTLET, and other times with a deserved respect, for instance Sherry Jackson's tough gangleader in STINGRAY or Joanne Woodward in WINNING. But in each of these examples and in nearly any other you care to mention the women are essentially along for the ride, and are not part of what is constantly being redefined as an exclusive male enclave.

———— The road movie therefore is virtually a locker room on wheels for men to indulge their camaraderie as well as their misogynist tendencies. The "buddy ethic", so prevalent in every conceivable type of commercial movie, is especially strong in road movies. Men are historically, although not necessarily naturally, the helms-persons of trucks, cars and motorcycles, so the high incidence of male role games in these films is to be expected. Most of the relationships between road men are, in fact, not much more dignified than those they have with the female characters they come into contact with. Confronted with challenges by the fact of their own neglect or misjudgement, these heroes' last (and often only) resort is to *drive* out of trouble; WAGES OF FEAR, VANISHING POINT, STINGRAY, CONVOY and DETOUR are just a few of the movies which support this claim.

The numerous outlaw bike gang films demean their main characters even further, their stereotyped gang leaders being little more than truculent schoolboys trapped in the bodies of neo-neanderthals. We can take them seriously only when the script calls for them to do or say something untypically human, and in this type of low-rent exploiter they are invariably humbled by the twee morality of their "ol' ladies".

But in some of the better conceived and written road movies, attempts are made to investigate, or at least observe the correlation between males thrown together behind the dashboard. Unfortunately men are less willing to express their feelings, especially with other men, so what usually emerges in these films are a series of disjointed or oblique comments which mask real sentiments. In movies like TWO LANE BLACKTOP or KINGS OF THE ROAD, where the male leads are both taciturn and/or "scarred for life" (yuck), the audience has to work hard to establish the truth behind the facade. But in lighter-hearted enterprises like THUNDERBOLT AND LIGHTFOOT, CANNONBALL RUN, THEY DRIVE BY NIGHT and SUGARLAND EXPRESS the affections and mutual support mechanisms are more openly displayed.

And so we find a great variety of relationships nurtured by the particular constraints of the road movie, whereas the ones between man and machine are fewer and simpler. I've already touched on car chauvinism – which might cynically be construed as substitute sex (but not by *this* writer) – but equally common is something far more casual, the transport being strictly a means to an end and readily discarded as soon as it falters. Viz. Clint Eastwood's rapid seque from car to ambulance to bike to, of all things, a tour bus, in THE GAUNTLET, or his straighforward theft of whatever's going in THUNDERBOLT AND LIGHTFOOT. Eastwood's pragmatism should, but won't, be applauded by psychologists who contend that an affection for one's car is a probable indication of stunted emotional development, one small step removed from the worship of graven idols. Yet no one blanched at possible unsavoury implications about a man and his horse, let alone A MAN CALLED HORSE!

But like any relationship, sometimes there are errors of judgement that can only be vindicated by violence. Take Ryan O'Neal as THE DRIVER, trashing a shiny new Mercedes in a deserted underground parking lot, a scene which brought the sado-machismo school of auto-eroticism out of the closet for the first time. O'Neal's particularly destructive behaviour supports a theory of mine which concerns the traces of zenophobia woven into quite a number of road movies. Consider for a moment how few heroes actually drive imported cars. Even in bike movies, where the patriotic option is limited to Harley-Davidson, a marque which accounts for less than seven percent of the total U.S. market, one rarely sees a Japanese or European machine... Unless, of course, its rider is being humiliated in a painful and preferably deliberate fashion.

This jingoism probably goes down as well in the executive suites of Detroit as it does in the cinemas of the mid-west, where "furrin' tin" is disdainfully dismissed as just that. This was emphasised to me when I saw VANISHING POINT in a flea-pit in New Mexico. When the hero, Kowalski, terminally despatches a maniacally driven E-type Jaguar, already the battered veteran of many such impromptu back-roads challenges, the audience whooped and cheered for fully sixty seconds. The impression left was that an irritant had been removed from somewhere it really had no place to be – the highways of America.

Was such a vicious, international joust a deliberate sop for nationalist prejudice? "Oh yes", admitted Sarafian with a candid smile, "it was just a little comment for middle-America to get off on."

Whilst it is true that auto-envy has no such parallel in the western – how many horses were imported from Japan in John Ford's hey-day? – hostility to outsiders of the human variety is commonly depicted in both oater and road movie. Indeed this was the main thrust of almost every bike movie made in the late 'sixties and early 'seventies: Either the Hell's Angels brandished their aggression at anyone who tried to approach or infiltrate their territory, or they simply took their angst on the road to Anytown, USA, and provoked enmity in the local and usually hapless population. Car-based films like MAD MAX II, THE CARS THAT ATE PARIS and THE CAR employ the same siege tactics and fears, but few films have articulated them as moral clashes to the same brutally effective degree as EASY RIDER.

In EASY RIDER, the narrow attitudes and intolerances of the deep south were revealed in all their ugliness, and eventually they caused the deaths of the film's protagonists. This was a kind of *volte face* on the usual biker-pic myopia, because the heroes were hippies rather than Hell's Angels. And although their demise was sudden and brutal, there was a kind of bitter logic to it, for EASY RIDER's vision of America was of a country in spiritual decline, where simple pride in humanitarian values had been insidiously overthrown by self-righteous bigotry. Jack Nicholson, in his wonderful portrayal of the drunken lawyer, George Hanson, commented sadly: "You know this used to be a hell of a good country. I can't understand what's gone wrong with it."

I suspect the reasons were lost on a lot of European audiences, too, the manner of Peter Fonda's and Dennis Hopper's deaths seeming barely credible. But we are forgetting yet another link with the Old West, the right of every citizen to carry a gun. As a consequence of this grim anachronism, we find chilling figures showing that even in an apparently enlightened 1980, there were 10,728 deaths in America by handgun alone, compared to just 8 in Great Britain, 21 in Sweden and 52 in Canada. In such a light, whimsical shootings by suspicious, mean-spirited red-necks have an air of crazy inevitability about them.

In VANISHING POINT, this same sad commentary on the mental health of the average American is reflected in Kowalski's revulsion towards the corruption he was supposed to condone, and preferably indulge in, during his previous career as a patrol policeman. It appeared again in the pent-up racism that finally exploded in a small town's attack on the blind, black disc-jockey, Super Soul. In the more carefully plotted road movies, police corruption often provides thinly veiled justification for outlaw tendencies, even extending to the actual murder of a cop or two. Sometimes this is treated as evidence of serious social malaise, as in THE GAUNTLET where by the time we reach the end of the final reel, it's almost taken for granted that the police chief is going to stop a few bullets, which of course he does. Generally, though, lawmen are treated merely as bumbling adversaries, such as Ryan Mitchell's crabby Chief of Detectives in ELECTRA GLIDE IN BLUE, or Ernest Borgnine's tritely bellicose patrolman in CONVOY.

But the frequency with which road movie characters dice with the law is not simply because they are social bogeymen, evil-minded or otherwise. It's just that they actually *do* appear on America's roads almost as often as stoplights and, as such, they provide a convenient relief from the tedium of driving that would otherwise render road movies theatrically impotent. Or as Paul Bartel explains:

"One of the great problems (with road movies), is that being in cars isolates people. That factor gets exaggerated in race movies like CANNONBALL, where the characters would be logically expected to spend most of their time in the cars, and so intercommunication between rivals is very difficult so you have to keep inventing reasons for them to stop."

And some are more plausible than others, the dutiful highway patrolman being an especially logical foil in a world where speed limits are made to be broken and the only difference between exuberance and dangerous driving is whether you get away with it or not. It's a sign of the times that our sympathies are rarely with the cops in a road movie, whereas in the average oater, the hard-pressed man wearing the tin star was invariably the hero. This merely confirms the shifting morality of a society that has lived with the abuses of power for so long that a diminished respect for authority is virtually a fact of life. But then, on an entirely superficial level, it's hard to love a man dressed up like a neo-Nazi fighter pilot when he pulls up in front of you on a gleaming, gadget-laden motorcycle. Only ELECTRA GLIDE IN BLUE has really attempted to show us what might lie behind the aviator shades and that infuriatingly well-pressed shirt. But because the central character, John Wintergreen, is such an obvious wimp and every other cop in the film taunts him mercilessly, we still end up feeling that the police are just short tempered subhumans in uniform.

But if the police are unfairly treated in road movies, what about the cars themselves! Apart from the obvious implication that there is no substitute for litres in a car chase, there is little detailed examination of the actual machinery utilised in road movies. Even in gauche deifications of vehicular might, such as STINGRAY, CORVETTE SUMMER or CANNONBALL RUN, it's evidently assumed that the audience is too technically ignorant to have any real interest in what lies beneath the bodywork. Since it's a hard core of car and bike buffs that have bestowed many of these movies with a cult status they could never have achieved on acting or cinematic quality alone, this is plainly not the case.

It would instead seem to stem from the directors' own attitudes to the vehicles involved, or as Bartel concedes, "I'm not particularly interested in cars as such, only in the action they provide."

Indeed in some road movies the only technical focus is one of absurdity. Take for example, the Japanese entry in Burt Reynold's coast-to-coast road race, CANNONBALL RUN; a mini car loaded with computerised gizmos. The goofy unpredictability of the computer and the voluble mania of the car's Nipponese crew – sub-titled throughout – betray yet more prejudice toward cars that are small and foreign.

Very occasionally, however, we come across a film where some genuine affection and appreciation, if not serious thought, lies behind an effort to dignify the glib iconography of car culture. A case in point is Monte Hellman's TWO LANE BLACKTOP, which successfully conveys the nervy, visceral thrill of illicit drag racing. Hellman quickly establishes the authenticity of his story, and elicits our respect for the deceptively drab '57 Chevvy that is elemental to the plot, by simply having its driver, James Taylor, glumly recite a list of tuning mods and special equipment. This is done by way of an awkward boast to the female hitch-hiker that Taylor and his mechanic pick up, one of the few social intrusions on their almost aimless quest for competition. This serves a number of purposes: it exposes Taylor's limited ability to communicate with a woman he'd like to seduce; whets the appetite of the committed hot-rod freaks who'd like to know just how it is that a dull, grey Chevrolet can demolish more ostentatious opposition whenever and wherever; and it offers the uninitiated a tantalising insight into the strange netherworld of back-roads drag-offs.

The inquisitive sceptic will find that this sub-strata of the motorsports industry still thrives in more remote parts of the States. Find your way out to the dimly neoned avenues of Taco Bells, all-night gas stations and 7-Eleven grocery stores that skirt some small city in Arkansas or Michigan. Make a few casual enquiries, carefully establishing that you are not an agent of the law or a vicarious idiot, but an out-of-state freak. Pretty soon some lank haired kid'll come burbling out of the shadows in a 427 cubic inch Camaro with a jacked-up rear end, fat tyres and "serious business" writ large all over it. You're a betting man, you say. You're interested in a little, ah, action. And if you pass for real, you may shortly find yourself on a deserted tarmac strip a mile or two away from the city limits, but in the company of some decidedly heavy traffic.

Fifty bucks on the Plymouth Satellite, my friend? A risky choice against the smaller, lighter but significantly less, um, modified Ford Mustang. But we shall hold your money and see what happens when the guy drops his handkerchief and the drivers bury their right feet in the carpet.

TWO LANE BLACKTOP captures the atmosphere of muscle car combatry rather nicely, although a slight tendency to turn one of the more important races into a sort of *Beach-Party-Goes-Drag-Racing*, somewhat undermines its conviction. Not a million miles down that same road, is Lamont Johnson's LAST AMERICAN HERO, a film based fairly loosely on the life story of six-time NASCAR champion, Junior Johnson. Jeff Bridges plays the boy who graduates from backwoods deliveryman for his father's moonshine liquor business – always a few car's lengths ahead of the local sheriff – to being the king of the 190 mph stockcar ovals. Johnson's sympathetic treatment of the righteous lawlessness of the old-timers who continue to operate illegal stills in the forest of North Carolina and Virginia, is complemented by the respect he pays the automotive side of things, particularly the preparation of Bridges' racing machinery. But perhaps because it didn't have Burt Reynolds in it, HERO failed to draw the audience enjoyed by another, less credible moonshining movie, WHITE LIGHTNING.

What binds BLACKTOP, HERO and some other movies like ROAD GAMES and LE MANS together, is their reverence for an attitude peculiar to their driver-heroes. This is partly an appreciation of of serious driving machinery, and partly an unspoken acknowledgement that their vehicle is jointly responsible for their status, even their personality. These are elements which through some odd symbiosis, ennoble both car and driver. Films which reflect this comprise a select sub-genre which are all the more worthy of the cineaste's attention, laden as they are with clues to the car culture of the 'fifties and 'sixties.

In the mid-fifties, teenagers were either given hand-me-down sedans by their doting parents, or bought them cheaply secondhand – disposability being the cornerstone of Detroit's marketing strategy at the time. Eager to cast off the mantle of austerity imposed by post-War economics, a new generation of teenagers developed a lust for speed and ornamentation that was most obviously expressed in the hot-rod and custom-car crazes.

But the instinct to tear apart an ageing family saloon, rebuild it with expensive performance parts and re-upholster and paint it in as outrageous a manner as possible, was one pursued only by those with a lot of money, or a dedication that prohibited any semblance of normal life. Most kids just bought what few custom goodies they could afford... and drove as fast as they were able!

Only a few movies were made that took the early days of car culture as the basis for a plot, and most of them were enjoyably tacky but bereft of anything in the way of a substantive plot or dramatic finesse. HOT ROD GIRL, DRAGSTRIP RIOT, HOT ROD RUMBLE and THE LIVELY SET were fairly typical of these time-warp tales. Minor pop stars in bee-hive hair do's and Ivy League suits, college dances and disapproving parents were the stuff such movies were made of, way before THE LAST PICTURE SHOW gave any depth to the lifestyle and emotions of the teenagers they were supposed to depict. Hot rod drivers were "kooks", their cars little else but gaudy mechanical freak-shows that were no more a threat to the status quo than they were to Detroit's car stylists. Hollywood merely indulged the dimly perceived fancies of the youth market, rather than explored them closely. Kids weren't taken seriously in those days, and on the evidence of what the hot rod films had to say, this wasn't surprising.

But by the mid-'sixties, things were starting to change, Elvis and the Beatles had opened up the market-place in a big way and the Ford Motor Company responded with a completely new kind of car; the Mustang. In trumpeting the concept of a "luxury personal sports car", Ford openly acknowledged the buying power of a young, style conscious, worldly-aware market. No other car manufacturer had dared do such a thing before and the only real performance car built in America up until

1964, was the ponderous, and expensive Chevrolet Stingray. The launch of the Mustang caused fist-fights and bribery in car showrooms all over the country, which quickly prompted other car makers to bring forward any tentative plans they might have had to cater for this new demand.

General Motors pushed its exotic, rear-engined Corvair, Chevrolet Camaro and Pontiac Trans-Am. Chrysler quickly rushed out their Dodge Charger/ Challenger series and Plymouth Roadrunner. And even the ailing American Motors Corporation produced a curious looking Javelin and AMX. Here were cars that would gargle a gallon of gas for evey ten or twelve miles of social irresponsibility on the freeway, but with cheap, home produced oil, who cared? The Mustang was originally conceived as the American equivalent of those cute little sportscars that affluent Europeans drove around in. It was smaller and lighter than most domestic cars of the period, but it had the V-8 engine and creature comforts that most Americans demanded. In those days, speed was a metaphor for high-living, and the Mustang and its ilk added a certain style to that illusion.

With the manufacturers themselves offering bigger and more powerful engines for their new brood of fantasy machines, the 'sixties soon became known as the age of the "muscle car". Extra-ordinarily swift in a straight line, though very much a tug-boat in the corners, a muscle car conferred instant status on its owner, and it was yours for around $2000.

"People would take the money that they'd been quietly saving up to spend on their first home", explains Paul Bartel, "and blow it on a car".

For many people it was their first love affair as members of the consumer society, and one that endures to this day. So it's common enough to see prematurely middle-aged men and women tooling around town in the muscle cars they owned in their teens. It's as if they're unable to let go the past remnants of their individual dream... a last link, perhaps quite literally, with the virginity they lost on the back seat. Glossy magazines and fat advertising catalogues cater to the tens, perhaps even hundreds of thousands who keep the faith and keep them running. And for every one die-hard 'sixties car freak, there are a dozen more who sit behind the wheel of their sensible Toyota or Ford Fiesta and wish for...

Well – wish for whatever in the world they want, the brazen image-mongering of the U.S. automobile industry and its advertising agencies having long since justified any brooding lust in the heart of any kid old enough to read something rude into the shape of a gear change lever. So at its most elementary, the road movie simply ratifies ideas already implanted by commercial interests, maybe adding a patina of cultural chauvinism for good measure: get in this large, sexy-looking car; drive fast; seduce women; gain freedom, be a hero whatever the odds.

But, as should be fairly obvious by now, that's only a beginning. Whether it remains as undemanding as a wham-bang action flick, or is cast in the mould of a latter-day romance or morality play set behind a dashboard, the road movie can be as versatile as a western. And like the western, there are a number of clearly defined sub-genres which merit individual scrutiny such as bike movies, racing movies, truck movies and the road movie as science fiction.

For the purpose of this book, I'm treating the latter category rather perfunctorily. Most sci-fi road movies are either high-tech melodramas that couldn't really afford the high-tech, or feeble attempts to modernise the chase film. In either case, these movies tend to rely for effect on the glueing of a few fibreglass fins to the bodywork of Volkswagen beach buggies, and similarly ludicrous diaphanous costumes to the females of the species. The compassion we're supposed to feel for new world buccaneers in films like MAD MAX (I or II) or DEATHRACE 2000, dissolves into laughter at the cheapness of their surroundings. In fact The-Last-Free-Man-On-Earth syndrome is better handled in more static sci-fi melodramas such as SOYLENT GREEN and ESCAPE FROM NEW YORK, where the budget for scenery and props can be concentrated in relatively few locations. Anyway, such confrontations between moralities old and new are the staple of countless futuristic B-movies, and it's in an encyclopedia on that subject that witless excursions like DEATHSPORT and SURVIVAL RUN belong, alongside GALAXINA and PLAN 9 FROM OUTER SPACE.

(I can defend the importance attached to DEATHRACE 2000 in this book, because it *doesn't* rehash the goodie vs. baddie business at all. DEATHRACE 2000 is *bad* vs. *bad*, and the fact that it's set rather unconvincingly in the 21st Century is irrelevant to almost everything, except the opportunity it provides for everyone involved to camp it up to the maximum).

Then we have bike movies which, it is admitted, also occupy a rather narrow slot, both in the variety of their storylines and the quality of the resultant scripts. Motorcyclists were always the poor relation of the motorist, an image not helped by the downright malfeasance of the bike gangs who, although they represented an infamous 1% of the breed, attracted 100% of the publicity. This state of affairs was exacerbated by the technical stagnation of the embarrassingly small home industry and the British factories who, until the Japanese got busy in the late 'sixties, maintained a supply exclusive of large, noisy, unreliable and all-round anti-social motorcycles. Obviously the only people who either wanted, or could cope with these oily hacks were large, noisy and anti-social. *Ergo* bike gangs, and *ergo* bike gang movies. Since Hollywood found the combination of unsavoury behaviour and limited financial outlay irresistable (Hell's Angels never slept and always rode around in the desert), the film industry quickly bcame adept at producing quickie biker movies that almost completely misrepresented motorcyclists and their machines. These demand our humorous indulgence rather than any indignation over factual abuse, and in that spirit, how could anyone resist a promotional pitch like the one from American International's 1967 epic, BORN LOSERS?

"BORN LOSERS is more than a tough, hard-hitting drama of outlaw motorcycle gangs and their depredations against society. It is authentic. The producers based the motion picture on factual data concerning cycle gangs and other renegades who today run rampant through our society.

"Producer Dolores Taylor was determined that a movie had to be made depicting the strange apathy towards one's fellow man which had become so prevalent in America. BORN LOSERS is this picture."

Hilarious rubbish, and a turkey of a film to boot, BORN LOSERS was one of a slew of films that followed in the wake of WILD ANGELS, Roger Corman's seminal bike gang B-movie. Corman, having already made a name for himself with low-budget gothic horror and graphically violent gangster films, had dabbled briefly in road movies with THE YOUNG RACERS in 1963. Possibly because that particular film didn't offer him as much scope for gore and nastiness as his other work, Corman didn't return to four wheels until the 'seventies. But THE WILD ANGELS was far more fertile ground. Its crowded menu of outlaw intrigue, sex, drugs, and nihilism is discussed at length later in this book, but it's worth pointing out that almost all of the cycle gang films that succeeded it, failed to find any wider terms of reference.

Only when it went beyond the realm of the outlaw biker did a motorcycle movie begin to get a grip on reality and the notion of what makes a film worth watching. The few directors who've bothered to make this quantum leap have almost always landed at the race track, which isn't all that surprising, for the darting, weaving gyrations of the biker racer provide an impressive dramatic focus of their own. Documentaries like ON ANY SUNDAY (I & II) prove that there are no serious technical limitations in capturing this on film, but when Hollywood pumps bucks into a rare foray into fictionalised bike racing, it not only falls short of conveying a vivid impression of what life is like when you start drifting sideways on a steeply banked motorcycle at 150 mph, but also denudes its central characters of any real credibility. Sidney Furie's orgy of back projection in LITTLE FAUSS & BIG HALSY was not, for example, redeemed by Robert Redford stumbling about trying to look butch and enigmatic with a tooth-brush permanently stuck in his mouth. (Maybe the bristles got in the way of his lines?)

14

And if discussing these films in a wider context, it should be noted that their preoccupation with the silly posturing of their uniformly unbelievable characters, almost disqualifies them from the category of racing movies altogether. In films that use the race track as a scenario for any level of drama or comedy, there must always be a compromise between thespian antics and thrills and spills on the tarmac. Relentless shots of looming corners and tense moments as Jean-Claude Whatsit takes the lead from the bankrupt cripple in whom the audience's hopes are invested are all very well, but they soon become tedious if they're unrelieved by some action beyond the circuit itself. *And the quality of one has to be high enough to justify the existence of the other.*

Despite some stunning camera-work, John Frankenehimer's GRAND PRIX is an example of just such a failure, as is the Al Pacino mistake, BOBBY DEERFIELD. In both cases the storyline and acting are less absorbing than the car racing, and so they both fall flat on their noses and ultimately exist as little more than extended Martini commercials.

As in the better westerns (or indeed the better anythings) the authenticity of the surroundings quickly acclimatises the audience for whatever follows, even awkward dialogue and lumpen plotting seem to matter less if the action sequences are fast and furious and real. The racing footage in LE MANS and WINNING was, of course, largely shot separately from the actual combat: you just can't have millions of dollars-worth of blue-eyed filmstar swanning around between equally valuable racing machinery driven in anger before a paying public. But by carefully splicing film of the real and the mock racing together, a sense of occasion is created for the cinema audience, just as it is for the fans who trek their way into the countryside to watch these high-speed gladiators at work. This adds tension to the off-track dramas that DEERFIELD, LITTLE FAUSS etc., etc., largely try and make do without.

These are just some of the strengths a racing movie needs if it's going to rise above the cheap glamour that is its easiest option. And, on the subject of glamour, recent years have seen an increasing number of films eulogising the long distance trucker. Popular mythology would have us believe that the truck driver is the one, true upholder of the cowboy ethic and the pioneer spirit, and some of the analogies do hold water. Stopping only for food, gas and essential repairs, truckers are certainly a lonely breed. They meet only other drivers in the surreal, supermarket atmosphere of the truckstops that are their oases in a sea of fatigue. Like that of the bike and hot-rod gangs, this is a closed society that favours chauvinism and bigotry, but the difference is that the trucker lives out his fantasies via a steady stream of soppy country 'n' western music and Marlboro man-type commercial imagery. The trucker may just be an outlaw, but he's a white, middle American outlaw, and that gives him a certain edge.

When producers first saw the potential of freight haulage as movie material, it lacked the gloss of today's trucking business, and that makes these early films especially interesting when evaluating the sub-genre as a whole. WAGES OF FEAR and THEY DRIVE BY NIGHT are two of the best, the latter film helping Humphrey Bogart to side-step his typecasting in crime and gangster movies. Although the film uses a small trucking operation as its backbone, THEY DRIVE BY NIGHT's plot diversifies into a vicious romantic intrigue. Ida Lupino gives a wonderfully excessive performance as the witch of the piece, with George Raft and Bogart holding up well against her skullduggery. Bogart manages to lose an arm after falling asleep at the wheel and crashing his rig – something his fans must have loved at the time.

WAGES OF FEAR also used trucking, in this case a specific and highly dangerous journey, as an unconventional theme around which an "escape to freedom" plot unfolds. Neither of those films were made consciously as road movies, and both are that much better off for it. The emphasis here is on action and melodrama with a heavy dollop of tension thrown in to keep us all interested, but through nuance and careful attention to detail, the sheer physical strain of driving heavy trucks permeates throughout.

Only one contemporary trucking movie adequately shows this sort of pressure – Joseph Strick's largely ignored little classic, ROAD MOVIE. Despite the conceit of its title, much of Strick's film steadily counts the odds stacked against the independent trucker. Strick, whose family was in the haulage business, combines this litany of mounting debts, debilitating schedules and attritional regulations with a damningly bleak view of man's disrespect for his environment. The film's two driving partners travel through a landscape wasted by industrial excess and littered with the roadside ugliness that other directors have successfully beautified, a view of the world that burns itself into the memory as indelibly as any image Strick created in either THE SAVAGE EYE or ULYSSES. The arrival of a fast-fading highway hooker gives all three of the central characters a perverse respite from their gloomy toil. The eventual product of this chemistry is however far more disturbing than anything ROAD MOVIE has to offer in its earlier stages, a shocking catharsis for individuals seemingly adrift in a spiritual wilderness.

How different is the lifestyle of the modern trucker as depicted by Sam Peckinpah in CONVOY, where everyone wears a clean t-shirt, the trucks are always freshly washed and the plot is little more than a pantomime which pits honest truckers against corrupt cops. Any insights as to the likely nature of life at the helm of a big rig are lost to routine slapstick or Peckinpah's well-known fondness for slow motion violence and catastrophe. And yet Peckinpah proved in THE GETAWAY that he could enliven a fairly ordinary road movie plot with a canny mixture of dark humour and subtle tensions, factors notably absent from CONVOY which he made fully six years later. (And somewhere in the interim, the co-star of both these films, Ali MacGraw, forgot how to act, too!)

But if the reasons for these wild inconsistencies of talent are perplexing, it's even more paradoxical that the major studios are generally unable to produce successful road movies, whilst independent efforts invariably become cult favourites and provide good return on investment. This is particularly true of trucking films, for virtually all the outstanding titles in this category are in fact economy models. ROAD MOVIE heads the list of course, but following close behind are Steven Spielberg's DUEL, and ROAD GAMES, a little gem by Australian director, Richard Franklin.

Although different in practically every respect other than the fact of their trucking basis, all of these films draw their strength from carefully crafted, almost rhythmic crescendos of threats to a crumbling status quo. Two of these films, DUEL and ROAD GAMES, do actually use the same device to maintain this steady air of menace; an apparently driverless vehicle that all but kills off the hero.

The idea of a motorised bogeyman is also employed by Elliot Silverstein in THE CAR, but in this case, the forces of evil appear to win.

However, DUEL exploits the nightmarish idea of a runaway truck relentlessly chasing a jittery travelling salesman down lonely backroads, whilst ROAD GAMES reverses the process, and has a sinister black van provoking the Samaritan trucker into all sorts of misfortune.

In a commercial context, DUEL and ROAD MOVIES are also interesting examples of films that have prospered amidst the turmoil that's currently got a lot of the old-style movie moguls choking on their cigars. DUEL began as a short story by Richard Matheson which was published in 'Playboy' magazine. Spielberg read it, thought it would make a good movie, and tried to persuade his employers, Universal Studios, to put up the money. But as he explains, "They told me, 'If you can con Gregory Peck to commit, you can have a feature commitment.' Peck said no, and so we made it for t.v. instead."

This meant using an affordable actor, Dennis Weaver, who is best known as the t.v. detective, McCloud, and structuring the action around frequent advertising breaks. "The t.v. script was broken up into acts, where an exciting teaser holds your interest through a Clairol commercial," explains Spielberg.

DUEL was made for just $425,000, which included Universal's 25% studio overhead and sufficient extra material for a theatrical version of the film which Spielberg was convinced would be a viable proposition. Cinema International Corporation, which handled all Universal and Paramount product overseas, first sold the revised movie to European distributors. This, ironically enough, encouraged Universal to distribute the film to American cinemas after it had already played on television – the antithesis of conventional practice. To bring a movie in for that sort of money meant working to a tight, sixteen day schedule and shooting in continuity; that is in the same sequence as it's scripted. This is essential if you've only got one set of vehicles and you can't afford to damage a car or blow up a truck before it's supposed to happen in the story. Incidentally Spielberg had the same problem in SUGARLAND EXPRESS, where the script called for different police cars and sightseers to gradually build up into a huge procession of 300 cars winding their way through Texas. The biggest cost advantage of shooting a road movie is, of course, the fact that most of the action takes place on ready made locations, or inside a vehicle, so that continuity either doesn't matter very much or is easy to maintain. But filming each scene as it occurs in the story means that locations have to be carefully selected beforehand, and the weather has to be kind to a director working to a precise schedule.

CANNONBALL and DEATHRACE 2000 director Paul Bartel has a practical philosophy he applies to the problems involved in shooting road movies: "The film sequences never correspond to what is conceived in the original scripts. The physical reality of the cars and the streets and whatnot determine how the gags are actually shot. The attraction of this type of film is in finding solutions, compromises if you like, that work."

Made when Spielberg was barely out of his teens, DUEL betrays very little in the way of either luck or lack of confidence, and he claims this as a legacy of his television training:

"I think television is the best place to start because it disciplines the hell out of you. Television has taught me to imagine the finished product and then just before shooting, retrace my thoughts and follow that imaginary blueprint. T.V. taught me that, because you're making an hour show in six days, you'd better know it line for line, shot for shot exactly what you're doing. The minute you dissemble, you're behind schedule a day."

Proof of his efficiency is Spielberg's incredibly low ratio of shots taken to accomplish an acceptable print, just 4:1 in the case of DUEL.

Had the film not originally been made for television, it's fairly obvious that it wouldn't have been made at all, and as Spielberg himself says, "My advice to anyone trying to break in (to movie making) would be to write a script and bring it to the networks and say you want to make it for television. They *have* to buy so many movies a year..."

But if DUEL got a theatrical release through the back door of television, ROAD GAMES shows how an independently produced film can benefit from the collapse of the Hollywood infrastructure. Made by an Australian company and produced and directed by another refugee from television, Richard Franklin, ROAD GAMES won an American distribution deal largely because it boasted two medium-rate box office stars, Stacey Keach and Jamie Lee Curtis. Franklin's ability to get these actors to work on a low-budget Australian movie as much underlines the dearth of attractive roles available on America's west coast, as it does the growing reputation of Antipodean cinema. It also illustrates how the division between major studio and independent productions are becoming blurred by the economics of film making in the video age.

The big companies are now concentrating their resources on blockbuster productions which they make fewer of, but reap good profits from. This leaves their distributors with a paucity of films to put into the cinemas between the lavish moneymakers, a situation the independents have capitalised on by raising their own finance, attracting good, bankable stars and then selling or leasing exhibition rights to the majors. The risk to the big companies is minimal, the indies usually get most of their money back quickly, and the market enjoys a wider variety of film. This doesn't mean that no small and medium budget films are being made by the old guard, however. In fact many big studios are learning their lesson from the indies and creating independent-style production departments within their financial structure.

This is a healthy state of affairs for road movies, which achieve their cult status only after production costs have been defrayed by their commercial viability in the larger American cities. European audiences, for example, only get to see these and many other interesting American films because they've already made their money in America.

The same is true of the straightforward exploitation movies of Roger Corman and his ilk, whose appeal to road movie fans is their (apparently) unintentional campness. Corman understands his audiences very well, the working and lower middle-classes of the industrial areas who still go to the cinema for hard action and gore. To this end he maintains a strict regimen which requires his directors to pack in as much violence and mayhem as they can, and at the expense of the storyline if necessary. He also insists on "shooting the money", or concentrating as much as possible on the sequences that cost the most to film, and tinkering with the editing after a director has delivered the finished product.

"Sometimes," explains Paul Bartel, "he sends out a camera crew and shoots whole new action sequences in order to add or replace bits he thinks are necessary. Roger doesn't think that the identity of the director is that important, he thinks of himself as the real *auteur*, to which end he often disenfranchises the original director and 'saves' the movie himself."

Corman regularly keeps the soundtrack at a low level for the first few minutes of his films, so that after the projectionist has set the volume and gone off for a cup of coffee, he'll have unwittingly ensured that the audience's ears will be as battered as their eyes and minds are. Finally, Corman always keeps his films short, 95 minutes or less, so that he doesn't lose his audiences' interest and perhaps, as Bartel jokes, "So that they can be carried in just two film canisters... he even cuts down on transportation costs!"

Despite his reputation as a cheapie, it's important not to underestimate Corman's accomplishments beyond his mastery of kitsch. Many of the great directors of the 'seventies started out as editors, cameramen or second unit directors with Corman's company, New World Pictures. The list includes Martin Scorcese, Peter Bogdanovitch, Jonathan Kaplan, Frances Ford Coppola, Jonathan Demme and, of course, Paul Bartel. New World, and its distribution company, American International, also pioneered the market for cheap, unpretentious exploitation movies. This in itself was an object lesson to both the major studios and frustrated young film-makers, namely that the commerciality of a movie didn't depend on the size of its budget or the reputation of the actors involved.

Corman also nurtured some prime acting talent in a sort of loose-knit repertory company, most notably Jack Nicholson and Bruce Dern who were appearing in atrocious biker movies like THE REBEL ROUSERS and CYCLE SAVAGES, long before they graduated to more dignified enterprises. One of Corman's biking actors, Jack Starret, even went on to direct a couple of his cycle gang pics, RUN ANGEL RUN and ANGELS DIE HARD, the latter being written *and* produced in just three months so it could herald the launch of New World Pictures in 1970. Other names that crop up regularly in the exploitation car and cycle pictures of the late 'sixties and early 'seventies include Adam Roarke, Jeremy Slate and Tom Stern. Most of these names have been unheard of since; cynics might say that their careers were based on their ability to ride motorcycles rather than any thespian talents they might have had!

But then there is the curious, perhaps even pathetic case of Peter Fonda. A Corman alumni like Dern and Nicholson, Fonda has never really been able to break out of the biker mould. THE WILD ANGELS and EASY RIDER are still his best remembered roles, and since then he seems only to re-surface in road movies, like the unconvincing DIRTY MARY & CRAZY LARRY which didn't even have enough ambiguity to make it camp. Almost adding insult to his typecasting, was his cameo appearance in CANNONBALL RUN in 1981... as a bike gang leader!

Directors of those early, exploitative road movies generally fare even better than the actors who survived the ignominy of playing ape-heads on wheels. Of the Corman school, Bogdanovitch, Demme and Kaplan all went on to direct critically acclaimed work, some of which is detailed in this book. Their immediate peer group also includes Michael Cimino, who wrote and produced THUNDERBOLT & LIGHTFOOT several years before moving onto weightier matters, Steven Spielberg who had DUEL and SUGARLAND EXPRESS under his belt prior to developing an interest in deep sea fishing and UFOs, and Terence Malick, who established his lyrical visual style with BADLANDS, in 1973.

In a slightly different category – one with the air of the *avant garde* about it – we find Monte Hellman (TWO LANE BLACKTOP), Dennis Hopper (EASY RIDER and OUT OF THE BLUE) and Elliott Silverstein (THE CAR). These were directors with little or no real movie experience behind them (the exception is Silverstein, whose first feature, CAT BALLOU was a huge success and virtually re-defined the comedy-western), but a solid grounding in television. The speed and production values of the small screen were, as outlined earlier, an obvious attraction to producers managing a small budget, but the results often belied this. This is especially true of BLACKTOP where Hellman often went out of his way to set up shots that are more intriguing for their incidental detail than they are for their foreground action. Hopper, working closely with cinematographer Laszlo Kovaks, managed to create some special effects for EASY RIDER that were later adopted by numerous directors (e.g. flash-forward editing). Kovaks himself worked his way up from some of the most wonderfully tacky biker pics, through EASY RIDER, SLITHER and PAPER MOON to become one of Hollywood's photographic elite. Although he was a respected camera man in his native Czechoslovakia, it is rumoured that he had to pay his dues like this because he'd arrived in America without a union card.

But perhaps the greatest unsung heroes of road movies are the stunt men, and once again we find the same names cropping up again and again. Probably the three best known stunt co-ordinators are Alan Gibbs (CONVOY, CARQUAKE), Everett Creech (DRIVER, THE CAR, LAST AMERICAN HERO) and Cary Loftin (VANISHING POINT, DUEL, SUGARLAND EXPRESS). Of these, Loftin is generally regarded as the most unassuming, as Richard Sarafian attests: "I'd sometimes be in the car with him and he'd be chatting away about what we were going to have for dinner that night and then, without even pausing for breath, he'd suddenly throw the car into a perfect 360-degree skid! Still, I'd feel safer going round a corner at eighty miles an hour on two wheels with Cary, than I would going down to the grocery store with most people."

Spielberg, too, has nothing but praise for Loftin: "Cary Loftin was the single personality responsible for the crew's safety during the stunt work (on SUGARLAND). Cary takes every precaution imaginable to protect his people, and he hires the best stunt men. The most difficult crash sequence to stage was the night collision, and it was difficult to stage because it entailed a police car sideswiping our principal car, 2311. But it was a sideswipe that could only cave in the left hindquarters of the principal car because if it hit the door or the engine it could put the car out of commission. Cary told me he would drive the sideswiping car because it was the most delicate of all the stunts. And sure enough, he hit 2311 *exactly* where we told him he could. Also tied into that same stunt, and covered by four cameras, was Ben Johnson's car slamming into the local police car that had just sideswiped 2311, and that in turn is followed by ten Department of Public Safety cars rear-ending each other in true Rube Goldberg fashion!"

Although he's getting on in years now, Loftin still does the odd stunt job that appeals to him and runs a small Hollywood repair shop where he works only on the cars he likes. "He's a damn good mechanic, too," claims Sarafian. "We had three identical Dodge Challengers in VANISHING POINT, and they kept breaking down 'cause of the hammering we were giving them. Cary could work all through the night, cannibalising bits off them just so's we'd have one car running for the next day's shoot."

Although the precision required for many of the more spectacular driving stunts demands the services of a professional, some of the more colourful actors undertake as much of the hairy stuff as the insurance companies will let them get away with. Paul Newman and Steve McQueen did quite a lot of their own driving in their respective racing films, WINNING and LE MANS, and of course there is McQueen's famous car chase in BULLITT, which he is also reckoned to have done entirely himself. Sometimes though, as Paul Bartel explains, the director has to keep a careful watch on the zealous actor-cum-stunt man: "In several of the action sequences in CANNONBALL it was easier to let David Carradine do his own stuntwork, which curdled my blood a bit. In fact after that bit where he drives at full speed up the uncompleted freeway bridge and then skids to a stop just a few feet from the end, I had to put a stop to it just for my own peace of mind!"

So far I've frequently drawn on the similarities between the road movie and the western, but I hope the reader will appreciate that glibly lumping all road movies together as motorised westerns is hopelessly unfair. A more accurate definition of the genre is that it embraces almost any film in which a motor vehicle is elemental to the plot. This excludes films which may contain brilliant car chase footage, such as BULLITT or THE BLUES BROTHERS, but includes, on the other hand, movies like BADLANDS and THE GRAPES OF WRATH which use vehicles to transport the main characters from scene to scene but are rarely the subject of, or scenario for, dialogue in themselves.

If this widens the parameters of the road movie, and I'm sure it does, then it's rather surprising that so few European directors have tackled the subject, still fewer with any great success. The most self-conscious attempt to meld the requisite imagery was ex-movie critic Chris Petit's RADIO ON. This was a very British odyssey with a soundtrack that betrayed the awkwardness of British place names – you just can't turn the A40 into Chuck Berry's "Route 66" – and frequent allusions to the neo-German cinema of Fassbinder, Wenders, et al. To the road movie buff, RADIO ON's stylistic catholicism was a disappointment, for it failed to recognise the considerable success television has had in reflecting the character of Britain and its people. But Mr. Petit is a self-confessed disciple of Wim Wenders, and I suppose it was therefore inevitable that his film has some of the bleak, dreamy qualities of Wenders' own KINGS OF THE ROAD, as well as some rather unresolved elements of revolutionary cinema polemic.

KINGS itself is a real cineaste's indulgence, the story of a travelling cinema projector engineer with a passion for his work that renders him an obsessive and ultimately lonely man. He picks up a refuge from a broken marriage, and the two men's journey together turns out to be not so much the sort of "buddy saga" that is commonplace in road movies, but rather an essay in the despair of non-communication. Overly long and lacking much in the way of levity, KINGS OF THE ROAD is perhaps all we can expect of a German road movie. But to claim that foreign language and customs control somehow thwart the notions of easy escape or aimless travel that lie at the core of a road movie, is to ignore the Godard classics, WEEKEND and PIERROT LE FOU. Small budget, self-consciously *avant garde,* these are probably the two most successful expositions of the Eu-road movie, and it's perhaps not coincidental that one of the best truck movies bar none, WAGES OF FEAR, is also of French origin.

But taken as a whole, and with some quite dreadful efforts like HELL DRIVERS, SILVER DREAM RACER, THE LEATHER BOYS and GIRL ON A MOTORCYCLE to add to the list, European road movies are hardly a distinguished bunch. Maybe in the fullness of time, someone will follow Sergio Leone's example and simply treat Spain and Italy as low-cost alternatives to California... roll on the first 'spaghetti road movie!'

But for the moment we can only savour a body of work that is predominantly American and, in my opinion, profoundly important in the development of modern cinema. To this end, I've assembled the bulk of the road movies made since the 'thirties and arranged them alphabetically by title in the following pages. My own personal assessments of the relative merits of each movie accounts for the disparities in coverage. Thus THE DRIVER and TWO LANE BLACKTOP are, for example, accorded far lengthier analysis and description than, say, DRAGSTRIP RIOT and TEN DAYS TO TULARA. I make no apology for this subjectivity, but invite you to make your own judgements at your local cinema or film society.

Unless otherwise credited, quotes from directors or actors in the movies I've featured, are taken from my own interviews.

ANGELS AS HARD AS THEY COME

Oh dear, what an embarrassment. ANGELS AS HARD AS THEY COME was the first film in a career that eventually led, via a string of exploiters (including Cloris Leachman's cult classic, CRAZY MAMA), to the much praised MELVIN & HOWARD, in 1981. Demme produced rather than directed this film – indeed it's arguable that *anyone* did, although co-scriptwriter Joe Viola is credited with that responsibility.

The story, such as it is, chronicles a belligerent encounter between 1½ motorcycle gangs in a disused western movie-set township called, I'm afraid, Lost Cause. The larger of the two outfits, The Dragons, are led by a psychotic neo-fascist (Charles Dierkop), who is defeated in a largely unseen bike race by The Angel's hard-bitten leader (Glen Scott). Shortly after this, two Angels are sentenced to incarceration and humiliation in an absurd mock trial. "Let the people decide," screams Dierkop, the people being a jury of blood-crazed acid casualties. The rest of the story crumbles into the requisite melange of violent revenge.

Of course there are lots of fights, schoolboyish female chauvinism, drug orgies, the usual "odd ball" characters, including a chap called Brains who carries a copy of Dostoevsky at all times, muddled hippie aphorisms and some hilariously gauche lines like, "Hey man, what works is what's right, you dig?" and "I dig him the way I dig stray dogs."

None of this is at all convincing because hardly anyone involved seems to be acting. I suspect the whole cast were a bunch of Viola and Demme's student pals who thought it would be fun to make a movie and, quite literally, went along for the ride. The only name that seems to have endured is that of Gary Busey, who played the lead in THE BUDDY HOLLY STORY, making a prat of himself as a do-gooding hippie.

USA	1971	90 minutes
Dir: Joe Viola		*Prod:* Jonathan Demme
Prod. Co: New World Pictures		*Script:* Viola & Demme

Cast incl: Scott Glenn, Charles Dierkop, Gilda Texter, James Inglehart, Janet Wood, Gary Littlejohn, Gary Busey, Cheri Latimer and Don Carrera

ANGELS DIE HARD

"The script is inarticulate, pointless and vulgar... practically everyone involved is unattractive and offensive... no-one knows how to act." That's how the Los Angeles Herald-Examiner's Bridget Byrne saw ANGELS DIE HARD, and although Ms. Byrne's review typifies the press' distaste for this breed of biker exploitation film, it doesn't give much credit to what is, in fact, one of the better examples.

Corman protégé Richard Compton both wrote and directed this harrowing tale of cycle outlaws wreaking revenge on a hick country town, following the slaying of one of their number by the sheriff. And he did it in just three months. This, as much as anything else, accounts for the film's weakness, but it's partially redeemed by some decent work by Alan De Witt as an over-worked undertaker, and Connie Nelson as the evil sheriff's squeaky-clean daughter. Arch Archambault's photography is a cut or two above the norm for this type of production, which, incidentally, was supervised by long-time Roger Corman side-kick, Charles Beach Dickerson. Dickerson had given Richard Compton his first break as a director; a $25,000 budget for a soft-core porno flick called LIKE MOTHER, LIKE DAUGHTER, which grossed $85,000 in one week alone in Los Angeles!

The worst thing about ANGELS DIE HARD as far as I'm concerned, is a wretchedly amateurish soundtrack which, if his reputation is anything to go by, was written and recorded on the change Dickerson had in his pocket at the time. That apart, it's quite a laugh.

USA   1970   87 mins
Dir: Richard Compton   *Prod:* Charles Beach Dickerson
Prod. Co: New World Pictures   *Script:* Compton
Cast incl: Tom Baker, Williams Smith, R.G. Armstrong, Alan De Witt,
    Connie Nelson, Cary Littlejohn, Carl Steppling, Frank Leo
    and Mike Angel

ANGELS FROM HELL

Former outlaw biker returns from Vietnam, takes up with old cronies, ditches wife, moves to another town, starts up a new cycle gang, meets stiff opposition from rival gang, falls for but cheats on "go-go bar" proprietoress, engages in final shoot-out with rival bikers and cops, dies in conflict with the very establishment he sought to defend in Vietnam.

Yes, here we have a cycle gang movie with a moral paradox at its denouement, and a faint nod toward the pacifist sensibilities of the times. For all that, ANGELS FROM HELL is a fairly routine effort starring several names familiar to the genre. They include Tom Stern, Bob Harris, Paul Bertoya and some time biker-pic director, "Jumping" Jack Starrett. Female interest is centred on the coquettish Arlene Martel, a t.v. actress who had the distinction of playing Dr. Spock's wife in Star Trek, and who provides the film's best performance as the no-shit coffee shop boss. Direction was by ex-racing driver Bruce Kessler, whose previous experience behind the camera was primarily as stunt coordinator on BONNIE & CLYDE. This ensures that the movie has a certain realism to its hard-core biking action, and unfortunately, rather too much of it.

Giving him the benefit of the doubt, Kessler probably made the best he could of Jerome Wish's script, which lacks very much in the way of gravity or, for that matter, humour. And on the evidence of this film, Stern, as the rampaging Vietnam vet, had still to give a better performance than he did as the Chesterfield man in the early cigarette commercials!

USA   1968   86 minutes
Dir: Bruce Kessler   *Prod:* Kurt Newman
Prod. Co: Fanfare Films   *Script:* Jerome Wish
Cast incl: Tom Stern, Arlene Martel, Ted Markland, Steven Oliver, Paul
        Bertoya, Bob Harris, Jack Starrett, Jimmy Murphy and Sandra
        Gayle

IN COLOUR

BACKFIRE

Now this is a generic rarity; an exploitation film *à la France*. BACKFIRE
brings together Jean Seberg and Jean-Paul Belmondo, a team who enjoyed great
European success in BREATHLESS? and a well-known character actor, Gert Frobe,
playing approximately the same evil tyrant with a pathological craving for precious
metals that he'd recently brought to life in *Goldfinger*.

The plots finds Belmondo as an up-and-coming journeyman crook, who's
hired by Frobe's sinister organisation to drive a shipment of gold from Beirut to
Naples, where it can apparently be sold for 150 million. The currency of this 150
million is not revealed, but we are told that the metal has been cunningly fashioned
into the body of a Triumph sports car Belmondo is to use for the trip, and so Ms.
Seberg is sent along by Frobe to see he doesn't try and abscond with the motorised
swag... which of course he does. He also dallies romantically with his chaperone, who
must be the only Frenchwoman with an Iowan accent, but she's a double-dealing little
minx and shops him to Frobe.

BACKFIRE fails as melodrama for a number of reasons not entirely
unconnected with Belmondo's determination to play the squishy-nosed Gallic enigma,
and at the expense of his ministrations to Ms. Seberg. As a pair of amorous tykes on a
European jaunt, they just don't seem to have their hearts or minds on the job. And the
snatches of wry humour thrown in here and there aren't self-deprecating enough to lift
this medium-budget film on to the same plateau as the conspiracy theory spoofs it tries
to ape, specifically the James Bond series.

The director, Jean Becker, is the son of the famous French film-maker,
Jaques. Obviously he still had to learn that three stars and a bunch of pretty locations
do not necessarily bust the box office.

24

France   1965   97 minutes
Dir: Jean Becker   *Prod:* Paul-Edmond Decharme
Prod. Co: Royal Film   *Script:* Didier Goulard, Maurice Fabre and
                                                    Jean Becker
Cast incl: Jean-Paul Belmondo, Jean Seberg, Gert Frobe, Fernando Rey,
              Diana Lorys and Renate Ewert

BACK ROADS

Not to be confused with the Australian movie of the same name, BACK
ROADS let Sally Field capitalise on her role as a liberated, but soft-centred activist in
NORMA RAE, (and one she virtually repeated in ABSENCE OF MALICE). Here she plays
a brittle edged prostitute, on the run with a raggedy ex-boxer, Tommy Lee Jones
(unfortunate type-casting). As Amy Post and Elmor Pratt (unfortunate name), they are
constantly making or stealing a bit of cash, only to almost immediately lose it. Their
odyssey is given a smidgen of poignancy when we learn that Amy has a baby son who
has been put into care due to her unfitness as a mother. And what scrapes they get
into! Amy is nearly raped by a sailor, Elmor rescues her; Amy falls foul of a vindictive
brothel owner in Texas, Elmor rescues her; Amy puts herself up for auction in a rowdy
bar; Elmor rescues her. And of course it all ends happily when the couple realise the
error of their illegal ways and set off for California where Amy aspires to an honest
living as a manicurist!

Like the other BACKROADS, this is an annoyingly incomplete film which
fails to work on any of the levels it sets out to reach. The sort of acerbic romance that a
Bogart and a Bacall could carry off so brilliantly demands better actors and a less
self-consciously seedy atmosphere than the one created by director, Martin Ritt. And
Elmor's suspicions of Amy's desire for respectability and the return of her son is a
theme lacking either resolution or coherence. It also jars with her response to the
sailor's drunken taunts: "A whore is a sixteen year old with a bad reputation," she snarls
proudly, "I'm a *hooker!*" Even as a contemporary road movie, BACK ROADS palls in
comparison with, say, Joseph Strick's ROAD MOVIE, for Ritt and designer Walter Scott
Herndon persistently try and turn the squalor of the roadside scenery into something
charming and attractive, instead of showing it up for what it really is. BACK ROADS is
just too cute by half.

USA   1981   95 mins
Dir: Martin Ritt   *Prod:* Ronald Shedlo
Prod. Co: Meta-Films Assoc.   *Script:* Gary Devore
Cast incl: Sally Field, Tommy Lee Jones, Miriam Colon, Barbara
              Babcock, Nell Carter, David Keith and Dan Shor.

BACKROADS

In his first film as a director, Australian scriptwriter Philip Noyce offers a
rather uncertain social commentary on the plight of the aborigine, wrapped around a
road movie storyline.

BACKROADS brings together two strangers – one an aborigine just released
after a night in jail, (played by aboriginal rights activist, Gary Foley), the other a rather
shabby white drifter, Jack King (Bill Hunter). They steal a Pontiac together, then some
new clothes and some booze, collect Gary's Uncle Joe (Zac Martin) from the
government's aborigine "reserve", and take off on the lam. Out on the road, they pick
up a French tourist, Jean-Claude (Terry Camilleri), and Anna (Julie McGregor), the
daughter of a shop-keeper who refuses them service. As Gary and Jack trade nihilistic
homilies in the front of the car, Anna and Jean-Claude make love in the rear... and

Uncle Joe gazes laconically out of the window. Eventually they reach the ocean, something Uncle Joe has never seen in his life, and is ridiculed by Gary as he hesitates to walk toward it. Jack and Gary then find a Mercedes, and Joe instinctively shoots its owner when he finds them tampering with it. The trio are subsequently arrested, but Gary is shot by the police when he tries to flee.

Although some of the roadside scenes in BACKROADS graphically illustrate the humiliation suffered by the black Australian, Noyce rarely elaborates on this in his script. Only Jack's racist jokes callously allude to the aborigines' dilemma, and introducing Jean-Claude as a "real" outsider who in fact enjoys a better deal from life than the incumbent aliens, is an equally half-hearted way of making a point. The only real expression of resentment comes from Gary who spits out, "Enjoy *my* country", as he ejects Jean-Claude from the car for his sleazy behaviour. The character of Uncle Joe is underplayed, too. He comes over as being a victim of repression who's learnt to live with it, but there's little insight beyond that.

Backroads is, in fact, a generally unsatisfactory movie when it could've been an unsettling one. Its road movie gambits are thoroughly predictable and its social values obscured by bland presentation and an ill-considered screenplay.

Australia   1977   59 minutes
Dir: Philip Noyce   *Prod:* Noyce
Prod. Co: Backroads Prods.   *Script:* Noyce and John Emery
Cast incl: Gary Foley, Bill Hunter, Zac Martin, Bill Hunter, Julie McGregor, Essie Coffey and Alan Penney

BADLANDS

Including BADLANDS in a treatise on road movies rather stretches a point, for it's only in the last third or so of the story – as the two fugitives flee towards Montana – that the film embraces any of the elements normally associated with the genre. Its inclusion is justified for two reasons: Firstly, BADLANDS' cinematography set standards aspired to by many road movies made subsequently; secondly it is an example of that extremely rare bird, a narrated melodrama. These two factors alone render BADLANDS a unique and important film.

The story, based on the true exploits of Charles Starkweather and Caril Fugate in 1958, begins just after Holly (Sissy Spacek) and her father (Warren Oates) have re-located to Fort Dupree, South Dakota, following her mother's death in Texas. 25 year-old Kit Carruthers (Martin Sheen) drops into her life from his garbage collecting round and during an awkward courtship, draws utter contempt from father, who shoots her pet dog as punishment for her disobedience. Kit persuades Holly to run away with him and when her father forbids her to leave, Kit shoots him with a revolver, dumps the corpse in the cellar, and sets the house on fire. We are treated to our first sight of his naive logic when Kit cuts a combined confession/suicide message in a do-it-yourself record booth, and leaves it by the blazing pyre. The two fugitives run to a forest, build a tree house and virtually live on berries and birds' eggs until some bounty hunters materialise. Kit, the little devil, traps and shoots them, and at this point the film gathers momentum. The couple initially flee to a remote cottage occupied by Cato, one of Kit's erstwhile garbage collecting chums. But he decides the quality of friendship is strained when he senses Cato is likely to turn them in, so he shoots him. As Holly casually asks the slowly expiring Cato what death feels like, he receives a couple of young visitors. Naturally Kit shoots them to escape to Montana. En route they stop off at an opulent mansion, holding the owner and his blind maid hostage whilst they casually select essential provisions for their flight, including the rich man's Cadillac. By the time they near Montana, Holly has become alienated by Kit and his homicidal fantasies. With a police helicopter on their tail, Holly refuses to go with Kit when he tries to swop the Caddy for an oil-rig worker's truck. Now minus his psychological crutch, Kit is chased by a police car and, apparently tired of running, shoots his own tyre to allow them to catch up. The last scene is at an airfield where a huge detachment of national guardsmen surround Kit as he waits in custody for the 'plane to take him away, ultimately to the electric chair.

The problem with BADLANDS is that, although it's a distinctively made film, sometimes breathtakingly so, it is also unashamedly derivative. Kit's dispassionate killings, his implied sexual impotency and his muted respect for authority conjure up an image of James Dean. The conceit is emphasised when one of Kit's arresting officers actually says as much. Holly's easy neglect of the homicidal horror that she's a party to is strongly reminiscent of Faye Dunaway's role in BONNIE & CLYDE. Indeed the entire film extrapolates from several films chronicling the exploits of semi-professional killer-fugitives, including GUN CRAZY, THE HONEYMOON KILLERS and, of course, Arthur Penn's BONNIE & CLYDE.

All of these films offer only the thinnest excuses for their protagonists' murderous tendencies, but BADLANDS' use of a narrated storyline would, you'd think, provide an excellent opportunity to provide an insight into the workings of such troubled minds. But it's one director/scriptwriter Terence Malick ignores: Sissy Spacek's calm, atonal discourse only jars with the carnage on the screen when its past-tense recollections pre-empt or parallel a scene. (Interestingly, Spacek's talent for this type of work was employed a few years later in HEARTBEAT)

This failure to resolve any of Kit's motives, apart from the obvious and unsatisfactory assumption that if someone got in his way, he would shoot them, is BADLANDS' most irritating aspect. Even his capture, with sheriffs and guardsmen variously complimenting and encouraging him as he waits at the airfield, practically asks us to exonerate Kit, but without offering any justification for doing so. Malick's amoral treatment of Kit and Holly's activities is further exaggerated by the dream-like quality of the photography, art direction and soundtrack. Using wide angle panoramas and a lot of loose-mounted camerawork, cameraman Brian Probyn also pushed the film a stop, even for sun-lit daylight shots, "as a matter of routine", according to Malick, "Our only real departure was to over-expose the film a bit, then print down. Which further minimises the need for lights by giving you more detail in the shadows than you would have at normal exposure. The saturated colour came from our not flashing the film or using any filtration."

Malick also paid a lot of attention to colour co-ordination and visual irony: Holly's blue dress merging into the eerie green interior of her father's house; father painting a billboard showing a pastoral scene, the billboard itself sited in the middle of a pastoral scene; the dust-sheeted interior of the rich man's house contrasting with the black clothes worn by him and his maid; the bloody carnage in an idyllic woodland glade and, more than anything else, the landscapes. For the most part, these are shot from low down to maximise the impact of the vivid blue skies through which Kit and Holly slice in the Cadillac and Studebaker. Although you can't help but feel a sense of *deja vu* when you see these images, Malick denies you the time to stop and try and place them. The stream of visual seduction is so relentless that questions of plagiarism are soon forgotten, if not actually made redundant by the sheer skill displayed in the film's assembly.

The same could be said of the soundtrack which, if judged in isolation, would be annoyingly pretentious. In the main it consists of avant garde classics from the likes of Eric Satie and Carl Orf mixed up with arch pop song commentaries, such as Mickey & Sylvia's 'Love is Strange', and Nat King Cole crooning 'The Dream Has Ended' over the car radio as the couple speed through the night to their final destiny.

But you can't really hold any of this against Malick, knowing that and ideas of structure he borrowed were at least borrowed lovingly: he was a full-time fellow of the American Film Institute prior to making BADLANDS, and he obviously used his time there well. Malick also had scriptwriting experience, having worked on screenplays for DIRTY HARRY and POCKET MONEY, and the overall power of BADLANDS owes much to his habit of writing camera moves into the script. "It forces you to visualise the scene," he explains. "And if you can't visualise it easily, if you can't imagine where the camera would go, it's probably not a good scene."

BADLANDS, despite taking two years to complete, is an object lesson in low-budget, on-location movie-making. Shooting entirely in Colorado, Malick pared costs by borrowing Film Institute equipment, using a skeleton crew and, when money was running low, he broke off and did some commercial screenwriting. When the script called for a visitor to interrupt Kit and Holly at the rich man's house, Malick saved the cost of flying in a Hollywood actor by playing the part himself. And wherever possible Malick used non-professionals for the bit parts, especially in the case of the lawmen who close in on the fugitives in the film's closing stages.

"I was particularly happy with the performances of the cops," recalls Malick. "They tend to make better actors than the local people from the little theatres. They are used to dealing authoritatively with people, and they aren't intimidated by the camera. They just get up and say their lines and that's that."

Financed like a Broadway play by bringing together a lot of small, $1000 to $25,000 investors, BADLANDS was made for under $500,000 and was a success that Malick never quite repeated, even with a blank cheque from the Hollywood gnomes. BADLANDS may not, in retrospect be a great road movie, nor even a great movie *per se*, but it retains its milestone status for its craft, evocation and economic accomplishments – creative and otherwise.

USA	1973	94 minutes
Dir: Terrence Malick		*Prod:* Terrence Malick
Prod. Co: Pressman-Williams-Badlands		*Script:* Terrence Malick
Photog: Brian Probyn, Tak Fujimoto, Stevan Larner		*Stunt Dir:* George Fisher

Cast incl: Holly – Sissy Spacek; Kit Carruthers – Martin Sheen; Father – Warren Oates; Cato – Ramon Bieri; also starring Alan Vint, Gary Littlejohn, John Carter, Gail Threlkeld, Bryan Montgomery and Howard Ragsdale

BOBBY DEERFIELD

Showing little of the talent he showed in THEY SHOOT HORSES, DON'T THEY?, Sydney Pollack couldn't make much of the Love Story-Goes-Motor-Racing script that Alvin Sargent drew from Eric M. Remark's weepie novel, 'Heaven Has No Favourites'. His vacillation resulted in a lush tour of the epicurean hotels of Europe, which might've pleased a few tourist boards, but makes for a highly disappointing movie.

The script starts well enough when one of Deerfield's team-mates is mysteriously killed in an accident and whilst visiting a survivor of the crash in a Swiss clinic, Deerfield meets Lillian (Marthe Keller), who has a lisp and a sort of cosmic will to learn more about Life. Lillian seems unduly anxious to seduce Deerfield, although from his impassive, inarticulate responses to her probing intellect, he has made it abundantly clear that he's only interested in racing cars... and dull as hell. ("Do you believe in magic?" she purrs. "No." "Destiny?" "No."). So disinterested in anything else is he that when a chunk of Lillian's hair comes off in his hand during their first night together, he merely pats it back in place and goes to sleep. The rest of the film follows Deerfield's vague attempts to relate to the terminally unwell Lillian, and drive cars fast. Even the potentially revealing confrontation 'twixt him and his secretary/mistress (Anny Duprey) fails to bring the man's character out of its cardboard box, and when Lillian finally snuffs it, he can barely muster a tear.

This is all a truly dreadful waste of money and Pacino's acting talents. He plays the whole thing with as much depth and energy as a man driving a bus, and any hope of light relief from the motor racing sequences is dashed by Pollack's refusal to identify other drivers and thus the sense of competition which can be Deerfield's only joy in life.

BOBBY DEERFIELD is little more than one long Martini commercial, I'm afraid.

USA	1977	124 minutes
Dir: Sydney Pollack		*Prod:* Pollack
Prod. Co: Columbia Pictures		*Script:* Alvin Sargent

Cast incl: Al Pacino, Marthe Keller, Anny Duprey, Walter McGinn and Romolo Valli

BONNIE AND CLYDE

Bonnie and Clyde puts a sugar coating on the cheerless image of rural America presented by THE GRAPES OF WRATH, but it shares with the John Ford film a sense of the degeneracy of the 'thirties, whilst concentrating on a story of spirit triumphing over circumstances. In that respect it works well, but only by gently distorting the Clyde Barrow gang, making them more glamorous and strange than they actually were.

Ex-con Clyde Barrow (Warren Beatty) picks up a hard-nosed but lethargic waitress, Bonnie Parker (Faye Dunaway), after she catches him trying to steal her mother's car. Disarmed by Clyde's astute summary of her small town circumstances, Bonnie dares him to rob a store, which he does, and the two of them take off in a stolen car to become ill-fated partners in crime. They spend the night in a farmhouse repossessed by a local bank and are interrupted from their shooting practice the next morning by the ex-owner, who's come for a last look at his old property before migrating west. In a touching scene, doubtless supposed to help justify a lot of what follows, Clyde hands the gun to the dejected homesteader, and his black farm-hand, and lets them savour a moment's revenge by shooting at the bank's repossesion board. After a fruitless raid on a small-town bank that's run out of money, they meet C.W. Moss (Michael J. Pollard), at a gas station, and asks him if he's cut out for a job as their driver/mechanic. Clyde again turns on the maverick persona you know he's still experimenting with, and gets the boy to rob the station cash register in order to prove himself. After more raids and an awkward bedroom scene in which Clyde confirms the impotence he hinted at after their first job together, the trio are joined by Clyde's older brother, Buck (Gene Hackman) and his highly strung wife, Blanche (Estelle Parsons). They rent a house together but before they get a chance to do any home-making, they are forced to shoot their way out of a police stake-out, killing several cops in the process. Now wanted for murder as well as a string of bank robberies, the gang make a precarious inter-state flight, their progress punctuated by a touching reunion with Bonnie's mother, and a couple of close-calls with the police. Eventually, Buck is killed in a police ambush and Blanche blinded, leaving the original triumvirate to make their way to a squatters' camp for help with their gun wounds. C.W. then takes them to rest up for a while at his father's house. But Ivan Moss (Dub Taylor) is not as easily beguiled by Clyde's (now failing) charms as his son was and, hoping to get C.W. off with a prison sentence, betrays the gang's whereabouts to the police. Their subsequent ambush in a country lane is famous for the balletic quality of Bonnie and Clyde's involuntary gyrations, their bodies caught in slow motion as the bullets hail down on them.

Arthur Penn's quasi-documentary style in BONNIE AND CLYDE is one of the reasons it so effectively evokes the doomed optimism and frail calm of the 'thirties – unwittingly creating a parallel for the 'eighties at the same time. Unfortunately Bonnie Parker's sense of high-fashion, the improbably educated mannerisms of the working class Clyde Barrow, and the gleaming newness of the cars they steal, all undermine the reality of the situation.

It's therefore left to Burnett Guffey's camera and the art and set decoration of Dean Tavoularis and Raymond Paul to create a sense of time and place. Guffey holds back and lets you see a small-town mainstreet long enough for it to have an historical impact, and the F.D.R. election posters and gas-station ephemera help authenticate the drama. But even then there is a degree of exaggerated nostalgia that rankles with the truth, although this is perhaps in keeping with the other source of the film's inspiration, the extraordinary relationship between the title characters.

To Bonnie and Clyde, robbing and killing is all part of some big romp, a fantasy of their own making which insulates and elevates them from the poverty of the era. They are besotted with the images they're creating for themselves, intoxicated by

their initial ability to get away with it, and reluctant to bow to the approaching come-uppance they know they must inevitably face.

Clyde seduces Bonnie in a lovely little scene in her home-town café, but with visions of herself as a rich, confident lady rather then words of flattery or affection. Clyde boasts to the evicted farmer, that he "robs banks", as if saying it makes it true... but he still has to clear his throat and stop shaking before he actually walks into a bank with a gun in his hand. Even his choice of C.W. Moss, brother Buck and the increasingly hysterical Blanche as accomplices betray Clyde's sophistry, which of course, inures our sympathy for their criminal actions.

The streak of vulnerability that ultimately destroys them is twinned with a compassion they demonstrate toward the depression victims they meet; the ousted farmer and his family, the hopeless squatters, and Bonnie's mother, a thin, harried old woman who looks forward to nothing but a further deterioration in her circumstance, and the inevitable death of her only daughter.

"Well times is hard," mutters Buck as they view the paltry spoils of one haul, an excuse that almost condones their lifestyle as an economy and encourages many hitherto law-abiding citizens to drift into the crime of survival.

Penn's tendency to create fantasy worlds of his own (e.g. MICKEY ONE, which also starred Beatty, and THE CHASE), is held in rein rather more tightly in BONNIE AND CLYDE, and one must applaud his avoidance of artifice in building an atmosphere of pervading doom which begins after the first robbery and gathers momentum toward the film's bloody denouement. Guffey is an essential part of this process, for the early scenes are mostly light and sunny, reflecting the sense of romantic adventure suggested by David Newman and Robert Benton's script, but gradually give way to darker shades and images. Sometimes he makes the point a little more directly, for example the scene in which Clyde chases Bonnie through a summery field, catches her in an apparent recovery of his sexuality, and then suddenly the sun blots out the clouds and everything becomes gloomy.

Overall the temptation to sensationalise the subject matter is largely resisted, and the film works as well as a tragic love story as it does a thriller.

Often emphasising their inherent paradoxes with mild farce, Beatty, Dunaway and to a lesser extent all the featured players display an empathy for their characters that compliments any efforts Penn may be trying to make, particularly in analysing their choice of this reckless, dangerous way of life. They give the Barrow gang a strong identity; picaresque, human and believable, just as the real (but much larger) gang apparently were. Any other historical inacuracies can therefore be easily forgiven.

BONNIE AND CLYDE
Dir: Arthur Penn   *Prod:* Warren Beatty
Prod. Co: Tatira/Hiller/Warner Bros   *Script:* David Newman &
                                          Robert Benton

Photog: Burnett Guffey
Cast incl: Clyde Barrow – Warren Beatty; Bonnie Parker – Faye Dunaway; C.W. Moss – Michael J. Pollard; Ivan Moss – Dub Taylor; Frank Hamer – Denver Pyle; Buck Barrow – Gene Hackman; Blanche – Estelle Parsons

BORN LOSERS

Hard on the heels of THE WILD ANGELS, THE BORN LOSERS was quick to meet American International's frantic demands for graphically violent, outlaw biker pics.

The story – yes there is a story – was supposed to invoke criticism of public apathy and police lethargy as much as disgust for the gangs that challenged them, and it doesn't do a bad job in either department. Vicky Barrington (Elizabeth James) is a vacationing teenager who is raped and beaten by the usual gaggle of sneering animals with names like Gangrene and Crabs. The sheriff and his deputy (Stuart Lancaster and Jack Starrett), yield to intimidation of the physical kind when they begin investigating the ruckus, and compound their cowardice with the sin of shooting the only person who does have the guts to avenge the girl's honour, Indian half-caste Billy Jack (Tom Laughlin). Mayhem ensues.

The script, apparently based on a short story by Ms. James, is not unintelligent, and although obviously overblown, attempts to address a once topical problem. (Apparently a lot of this sort of thing went on in California during '66 and '67, probably a consequence of the free-love philosophy being taken a little too seriously by those who weren't getting any). There are also some touches of humour in BORN LOSERS; the blood from Jack Starrett's fatal head wound dripping down a James Dean poster, and the inexplicable appearance of Jane Russell as the mother of a rapee who actually enjoyed the experience.

But ultimately we are left with an excessively violent film which says nothing about the whys and wherefores of it all, only that it's terrible and nobody seems to want to stop it. It's far too long, at 112 minutes and the photography, although excellent in places, is marred by poor editing and focus jumps.

USA   1967   112 mins.
Dir: T. C. Frank (Tom Laughlin)   *Prod:* Donald Henderson
Prod. Co: Henderson   *Script:* E. James Lloyd
Cast incl: Tom Laughlin, Elizabeth James, Jeremy Slate, Jack Starrett,
        Jane Russell, William Wellman Jr. and Stuart Lancaster

BREAKER! BREAKER!

Produced as a dumb contrivance for Chuck Norris ('The White Bruce Lee') to show-off his prowess in the martial arts, BREAKER! BREAKER! has the distinction of being the only Kung Fu road movie. (Perhaps it should have been titled, 'Zen & The Art of Truck Maintenance'?)

Rugged trucker J.D. Dawes (Norris), goes to the rescue of his younger brother (Michael Augenstein), out on his first trucking gig and thrown into a red-neck jail on a trumped up charge. Dawes-the-elder gets word of this on his C.B. radio, whose coded slang gives the film its title, and races – inasmuch as one can race in a 40 ton truck – to liberate baby brother from the sadists who've imprisoned him. In order to give Norris as many chances as possible to physically destroy as many baddies as possible (he certainly couldn't do it with words), this involves taking on almost the entire population of the town.

Producer/Director Don Hulette also wrote the tinny soundtrack and he acquits himself in his various endeavours about as well as the featured players can act, i.e. badly. CONVOY, which was made four years later and employs a very similar plot, comes off like GONE WITH THE WIND compared to this.

USA   1971   86 mins.
Dir: Don Hulette   *Prod:* Don Hulette
Prod. Co: Paragon Films   *Script:* Terry Chambers
Cast incl: Chuck Norris, George Murdock, Terry O'Connor, Michael
        Augenstein and Don Gentry

C.C. & COMPANY

The best bit of this film is the opening sequence which follows Joe Namath through a supermarket. He rifles packets of bread, cheese, ham etc., makes and then eats a sandwich, buys a packet of chewing gum at the check-out and asks for trading stamps. From then on, it's all downhill.

Namath is a bike gang member who comes on like a boy-scout when several of his brothers try and rape Ann-Margret, who seems to be playing an itinerant fashion model. (It's amazing how the girls in outlaw biker pics always manage to look as though they've just spent the morning in a beauty parlour, instead of six days on the road eating raw animal flesh and indulging in unmentionable sexual pranks). Namath's samaritan gesture begets much naked writhing between him and Ms. Margret, and eventually to lots of gore and motorcycle action between Namath, gang leader William Smith and the rest of the chaps who abduct her and demand ransom. By the end of the film, Namath has seen the light and gone legit as a motorcycle racer. "How did you get involved with a gang like *that*," asks the incredulous Ann-Margret.

"I dunno," mutters Namath, "I guess I was just looking for something." (Yawn).

Unfortunately Namath hadn't learnt to act anything like as well as he'd learnt to play football, and as a start to a mercifully short film career, his unctuous delivery and unconvincing movements were hardly auspicious. He should have stuck to after-shave commercials, and Ms. Margret should've stayed at home with hubby Roger Smith, who co-produced and scripted C.C. & COMPANY.

USA   1970   94 mins.
Dir: Seymour Robbie   *Prod:* Allan Carr & Roger Smith
Prod. Co: Rogallan Inc.   *Script:* Smith
Cast incl: Joe Namath, William Smith, Ann-Margret, Jennifer Billingsley, Don Chastain and Mike Battle

THE CAR

A film that takes the driverless vehicle allegory even further than DUEL, Elliot Silverstein's THE CAR effectively imbues his pressed-steel desperado with a real personality, no less than that of the Devil's agent.

From out of nowhere, a large black car appears in the remote desert community of Santa Ynez, Utah, and kills a hitch-hiker and some cyclists. Local police set out to apprehend the car, but one of their number is quickly mown down by the sinister machine which, much to everyone's alarm, is claimed by a terrified eye-witness, to lack a driver. The next victims are participants in a school parade, survivors from which are chased by the car to a local churchyard. An oath from Sheriff Wade Parent's girlfriend (Kathleen Lloyd), who's in charge of the kids, repels the car at the cemetery gates. Suddenly we know we're dealing with a motorised messenger from purgatory! To ram home the point (sic), the car ploughs into poor Kathleen's house and kills her, as an act of revenge. What's left of the local cops set out under Parent's command to try and lure the beast into a canyon where they plan to dynamite it. Although they eventually accomplish this, the film ends with ground level shots of a car's wheels driving dangerously fast through another city, accompanied by a horribly familiar honking... which leaves us to consider the grim portent of the devil's immortality, as well as a sequel.

The sequel never happened, for although Silverstein had two successful films under his belt when he made THE CAR, (MAN IN THE WILDERNESS and CAT BALLOU), it was a case of third time unlucky with the script. Dennis Shyrack's story was clearly full of the most lurid possibilities and many of them are efficiently executed by Silverstein and his crew, but the script he wrote from it is banal to the point of not even being laughable. (Rumour has it that Universal cut out even worse doggerel from the original version after adverse reaction at preview showings). If the action was as infantile as the dialogue, THE CAR might work on the level of camp, much like DEATHRACE 2000, but since the quality of the direction is high, especially Everett Creach's stunt co-ordination, the end-product is a compromise of ideas and imagery... and the audience happily applauds the car for knocking off all those bumbling idiots. Time after time the chance to cement a bond between the viewer and the beleaguered townspeople is wasted by the script: Sheriff Parent's cavorting with his altogether soppy school-mistress mistress; the other cops with their drink and marital problems. All this is soap-opera stuff compared to the dark aura of menace and intrigue that surrounds the car.

"The two questions under consideration from the very beginning of this project," says Silverstein, "were the identity – or lack of identity – of the driver of the car and the visualization of the car itself. We had a familiar device that suddenly started to behave as another human being might. So the guessing game followed – and it got to be very real on the set and not just in the script: Is there a human controlling the device? If not, what is – and why is it doing all those terrible things?"

Although Silverstein correctly cites these uncertainties as the kernel of the car's appeal, they are of practically no interest to the police force of Santa Ynez. Instead it's cameraman Gerald Hirschfield and the stunt team who try their best to maintain a sense of doomy foreboding based entirely on the car and its exploits. They tease us by taking the camera behind the windscreen as the car lines up another victim, focusing briefly on what *might* be a viciously distorted driver's torso at the scene of the car's (apparent) demise. But without a script to illuminate the fuller impact of this mysterious and homicidal intruder, their efforts are significantly undermined.

Despite its relatively poor showing at the box office, THE CAR will 'however' go down in history. During the making of the film, stuntman A.J. Bakunas claimed the world record for a prepared fall – 195 feet from a bridge near Zion National Park. Terminal speed was 105 mph when he hit the air-bag but, according to Creach, all

Bakunas felt was "a pat on the back". Which is more than Silverstein got for his troubles.

USA 1977 97 (cut from 99) mins.
Dir: Elliot Silverstein   *Prod:* Marvin Birdt & Silverstein
Prod. Co: Universal Pictures   *Script:* Dennis Shyrack
Cast incl: James Brolin, Kathleen Lloyd, John Marley, R.G. Armstrong, John Rubinstein and Elizabeth Thompson

---

CARQUAKE
DEATHRACE 2000

It seems logical to deal with DEATHRACE 2000 and CARQUAKE as a pair because they were not only directed virtually back-to-back by the same man, Paul Bartel, but also featured many of the same actors and crew. Even the plots bear more than a passing resemblance; transcontinental road-races offering rich rewards for the winning entrants, all of whom have murky pasts and are duplicitous by nature. As its title implies, DEATHRACE 2000 is set at the turn of the next century and offers a United Province of America the chance to release aggression pent-up by economic depression and futile wars with Europe (!), by watching national heroes battle it out across country in poorly disguised beach buggies. To satisfy the population's more feral instincts, bonus points are awarded the competitors for each innocent victim they mow down in their path; one hundred for a pensioner, seventy for a toddler, and so on.

DEATHRACE has two main contenders vying for the laurels, a four-tongued gangster, Machine-gun Viterbo (brilliant type-casting of a young-ish Sylvester Stallone), and the mysterious Frankenstein, who also happens to be the official government driver. Draped from head to toe in erotic rubber-wear, Frankenstein has apparently been re-built by a team of crack (ouch!) surgeons after previous years' crashes, crashes from which he still managed to emerge victorious. Much to Viterbo's loudly voiced chagrin, the serious money is on Frank, the people's hero. This tells us something about the sexual fantasies of the electorate, as well as the manipulative ruthlessness of their leaders.

Rushed to the track literally fresh from the operating table, Frank finds himself with a new co-pilot (everyone has them, they're good for traction on sandy

CARQUAKE

surfaces, fending off an adversary's bullets etc., etc.) called Annie. What he doesn't know, of course, is that she's really a member of a clandestine political movement, disarmingly known as The Rebels, whose intention is to disrupt the race, commandeer the television stations broadcasting this carnage nationwide and alert all and sundry to the terrible wrongdoings of the government who permit it. Naturally Annie falls head over leg-iron for Frank, only to discover that he has several identity problems, not all of which dampen her rampant idealism.

       The departure from this almost mortal coil of both wayward pedestrians and careless race drivers (to say nought of eager participants in Euthanasia Day at an old folk's home en route), is handled with the trashy zeal one would expect of a Roger Corman-New World production. CARQUAKE (a.k.a. CANNONBALL in America), is a rather different proposition put together immediately after the completion of DEATHRACE because, as Bartel explains, "I'd worked for over a year on that film and only been paid $5000 – Corman rarely gives his directors a piece of a movie. I had to make another picture quickly to get some money to live on, and although I had all kinds of ideas for films, I could only get people interested in financing another car action movie.

DEATHRACE 2000

       "Also, at that time the notion of a film about the Cannonball Baker Sea-To-Shining-Sea-Trophy-Dash was in the air around Hollywood. Warner Brothers were working on the GUMBALL RALLY, and there was even one somewhere in the works that was going to be made in the Philippines (adopts sonorous newsreader's voice) 'Where life is cheap!' Well I didn't really want to make another car movie right then, but I did want to eat, so I decided that I'd find a way to put more characterisations into it... have a bit of fun within what, once again, was a fairly straightforward action picture context."

Financed by Hong-Kong's Shaw brothers during their mid-seventies putsch to diversify away from martial arts movies, CARQUAKE was in fact a much slicker effort than DEATHRACE and largely devoid of ambiguous humour. Once again, David Carradine plays the hero, Coy 'Cannonball' Buckman, still smarting and on parole from his involvement in an accident which killed his ex-girlfriend. (In every Carradine road movie, there's a dark secret behind his tormented expression). Buckman is the fancied driver in the same highly illegal road race that provides the wherewithal for Burt Reynolds' CANNONBALL RUN (1981). And the $100,000 prize-money naturally attracts all manner of avaricious ne'erdowells, including Bartel himself as the mafioso backer of Coy's brother, Bennie, Sandy Harris (played by Mary Woronov, Calamity Jane in DEATHRACE), a young black chauffeur in his employer's Lincoln Continental (Stanley Clay), and a rather gross country 'n' western singer, Perman Waters, who takes his mother along for the ride and naturally has a deep-seated grudge against Coy. (Waters bears close resemblance to Rip Torn's cynically self-serving Maury Dann, the central character in another great road movie, PAYDAY).

CARQUAKE shares with DEATHRACE a story-line that would be unwatchably crass were it not for the enthusiasm with which director and cast hurl themselves – quite literally in some cases – into the fray. In both films endless rivalries are brought to brutal conclusions and with CARQUAKE, Bartel settled a few scores off-screen, too. As well as bringing in several ex-New World luminaries in bit parts (Johnathan Kaplan as a gas station attendant, Martin Scorsese as a mafioso, Joe Dante as a precocious punk), Bartel somehow persuaded Corman himself to play a district attorney determined to stop the race. By eliciting the enmity of entrants and audience alike, Bartel thus vilifies his old mentor for emasculating his creative efforts in DEATHRACE!

"It was one of the little compensations I was determined to give myself," explained Bartel. "Corman had cut a lot of the humour out of DEATHRACE because he thought it weakened it as a hard action picture which, in the end at least, is what he thought he could sell most effectively. I was originally interested in making jokes and seeing how the basic, rather grim idea of a race in which people were being deliberately run-over could be manipulated and made palatable. But the way Corman works is to give the director a free hand and a low budget, and if he's not happy with the result, which he invariably isn't, he sends out a second unit to add or replace bits he thinks are necessary. Roger doesn't think that the identity of his directors is that important, he thinks of himself as a real *auteur*, to which end he often disenfranchises the original director and 'saves' the movie himself.

"For example, Roger put blood in the final version of DEATHRACE, whereas I'd tried to finesse the killings themselves, so you got the satisfaction without the unpleasantness. I guess he didn't think subtlety would go down too well in Iowa!"

Despite his claims of butchery in the New World cutting room, much humour remains intact. The scene where the widow of one of the race victims is feted on a television chat show is a classic, as are lines like, "If they scatter, go for the baby and the mother", and The Rebel's preposterous ruse to paint a tunnel entrance on a canvas and suspend it over the edge of a cliff to which they divert the racers!

("Corman wanted to cut out that scene, he said it would be demeaning for what were supposed to be the world's greatest drivers to fall for a Warner Brothers cartoon trick like that. When I told him that it'd be a real crowd pleaser, he called that a specious argument... he really thought it should be an heroic action picture. Apparently he's thinking of re-making it as DEATHRACE 3000!")

CARQUAKE is a far more realistic film of course, its humour relying less on absurdity and goofy necrophilia than on contemporary racing iconography and road movie gambits... there's even a Trans-Am decorated in livery identical to Coy Buckman's, just to add some fiendish confusion and a few laughs. However, Bartel claims that with Corman's low budget, under $800,000, it was harder to make a sci-fi costume drama like DEATHRACE than the more straightforward CARQUAKE.

"For instance, in DEATHRACE, Corman got involved with the design of the cars, which looked fabulous on paper, but were ultimately made very cheaply, but that provided a joke in itself. In CARQUAKE, however, I couldn't afford to cheapen the vehicles or the stunt sequences. That big pile-up in the third reel was supposed to involve dozens of cars, but we had to use maybe thirteen or fourteen and shoot them with lots of cameras from different angles. And in several of the action sequences, it was easier to let Carradine do his own stuntwork, which curdled my blood a bit... expecially where he drives at full speed up the uncompleted freeway bridge!"

(The dearth of available automobiles presents a problem for many road movie directors, most of whom reflect Bartel's ingenuity in one way or another. For example Steven Spielberg has to destroy a whole used car lot in SUGARLAND EXPRESS, so he painted the few cars he had in a different colour on each side, then shot them with two banks of opposing cameras).

"The film sequences never correspond to what is conceived in the original scripts of movies like CARQUAKE and DEATHRACE," Bartel continued. "The physical reality of the cars and the streets and whatnot determine how the gags are actually shot. The attraction of this type of work is in finding solutions, compromises if you like, that work."

Arguably, Bartel's two movies work precisely because they *are* such glorious, unashamed compromises, and so one sincerely hopes that he'll find a backer for his bizarro horror-cum-road movie script, FRANKENCAR which on title alone sounds as if it's the inevitable conclusion of a terrific camp trilogy.

CARQUAKE

USA / Hong Kong   1976   93 mins.
Dir: Paul Bartel   *Prod:* Samuel W. Gelfman
Prod. Co: Harbor Prods (L.A.) and   *Script:* Paul Bartel and
       Shaw Bros. (Hong Kong)   Donald C. Simpson
Cast incl: David Carradine, Bill McKinney, Veronica Hamel, Gerrit Graham, Robert Carradine, Belinda Balaski, James Keach, Mary Woronov and Carl Gottleib

DEATHRACE 2000

USA   1975   79 mins.
Dir: Paul Bartel   *Prod:* Roger Corman
Prod. Co: New World Pictures   *Script:* Roger Thom and
       Charles Griffith
Photog: Tag Fujimoto   *Stunt Dir:* Ronald Ross
Cast incl: David Carradine, Simone Griffeth, Sylvester Stallone, Mary Woronov, Roberta Collins, Martin Cove, Louisa Moritz, Don Steele, Carl Bensen, Harriet Medin and Paul Laurence

CANNONBALL RUN

Burt Reynolds only seems to enjoy the sort of financial rewards the major studios expect of him when he's behind a steering wheel. But with CANNONBALL RUN, Raymond Chow's Golden Harvest company minimised the risk factor by signing up a plethora of box office biggies, largely for cameo roles in what is yet another coast-to-coast car race. It must be said that the film's storyline does actually have a ring of authenticity to it, for the Cannonball Baker Sea-To-Shining-Sea Dash that it follows was the highly illegal wheeze of sometime 'Car & Driver' magazine editor, Brock Yates. And Yates brings life to art by appearing here as the CANNONBALL RUN's organiser.

The highrollers who can afford to participate in this shambling farce all drive exotic machinery that will have the motoring cognoscenti drooling (Ferrari, Lamborghini, Aston Martin, etc., etc.), although the spectacular launching of Reynold's specially built *American* car early in reel one obliges him to take pot luck with an ambulance. The whacky japes that happen along the way involve Dean Martin and Sammy Davis Jnr. dragged up as Catholic priests, Roger Moore as an English nobleman who (get this film fans), thinks he's James Bond, and Jamie Farr as a Rolls Royce driving oil sheik. Peter Fonda has a small part as (and here's another one, film fans), a chopper-riding bike gang leader, and Bianca Jagger appears as a sort of wealthy, Bianca Jagger-type floosie.

Even though director Hal Needham accompanied Yates (who also hacked out the script), on the real 1979 Cannonball, his film subordinates realism in favour of slapstick, and even his slapstick invariably lacks conviction. The best bits in CANNONBALL RUN are Jack Elam's nicely deranged portrayal of the bleary, drug-abusing doctor Reynolds takes along with him to rebuff any patrolmen who stop him for recklessly driving an ambulance, and the final few minutes of the film which shows us takes that went wrong during shooting. This was an unwise move on Needham's part, for it proves that the gaffs and the ad libs were a lot funnier than the stuff they spent so much time and money on *trying* to make funny.

USA	1980	95 mins.
Dir: Hal Needham		*Prod:* Albert S. Ruddy
Prod. Co: Golden Harvest		*Script:* Brock Yates

Cast incl: Burt Reynolds, Roger Moore, Farrah Fawcett, Dom DeLuise, Jack Elam, Adrienne Barbeau, Terry Bradshaw, Dean Martin, Sammy Davis Jnr., Jamie Farr and Peter Fonda

THE CARS THAT ATE PARIS

Inspired by director Peter Weir's first incredulous contact with Parisian traffic, THE CARS THAT ATE PARIS is in fact about a once prosperous Australian mining town that now survives only by cannibalising cars. Unsuspecting motorists turn off the main highway towards Paris and are caught in vicious traps set by cheery townsfolk. The dead are disposed of at the town's hospital and the cars are stripped of their components by specialist scrap merchants. The women rifle any luggage they find, the teenagers rip-off the bits they need for their hot-rods. Altogether, it's a nice, energy-efficient re-cycling society.

George (Rick Seully) and Arthur (Terry Camilleri) drive into one of the traps and, miraculously, mild-mannered Arthur survives. Regarded as little threat to their colourful economy, Arthur is allowed to stick around and is given a job as a parking attendant, but in effect he is a prisoner. Arthur doesn't mind this, even when it dawns on him what the residents of Paris are up to, because he's never had a decent home of his own. So loyal is he to his new domicile, that he takes a stand against the delinquent hot-rodders, and this is the signal for gang warfare against the bad burghers of Paris. The town is summarily razed to the ground: the town that lives by the car, dies by the car.

THE CARS THAT ATE PARIS was the noted Aussie director's first feature movie and, despite a few seams that show the relative paucity of its budget, is a well executed and often hilarious moral tale. Friends Of The Earth must love it!

Australia	1971	101 mins.
Dir: Peter Weir		*Prod:* Jim and Hal McElroy
Prod Co: n/a		*Script:* Weir

Cast incl: Terry Camilleri, Rick Seully, John Meillon, Melissa Jaffer, Peter Armstrong, Edward Howell, Kevin Miles and Max Gillies

CITIZENS BAND (a/k/a/ Handle With Care)

If there's one piece of hardware common to the serious American driver, be he in a car, van or truck, it is not a particular type of gearbox, steering wheel or carburettor, but the C.B. two-way radio set. Of the two movies built around C.B., or Citizens' Band as it is properly known, Jonathan Demme's eponymously titled effort is by far the best. (The loser being BREAKER! BREAKER!).

Much like the films of Robert Altman, particularly WELCOME TO L.A., CITIZENS BAND is a kaleidoscope of sub-plots held together by a common thread, in this case the radio wavelength used by Demme's characters. These are the inhabitants of a sleepy south-western town who know each other better on the air than they do in real life. Or rather that their radio personalities are stronger and more clearly perceived than when they actually meet, separated as they then are from the technological umbilical cord that binds them together.

Nominally at least, the film's hero is Spider (Paul Le Mat), who runs a ramshackle C.B. shop and emergency rescue service. Spider becomes increasingly irritated by the incessant chatting of C.B. owners who abuse broadcasting regulations and tie up the airwaves, often delaying the help he offers to broken-down trucks. His solution is to turn vigilante, locate the loquacious offenders, and smash up their equipment. Thus we meet a spunky kid who boasts of his sexual conquests and calls himself The Hustler, the truck driving Chrome Angel, who keeps two homes with a wife in each, Dallas Angel (Ann Wedgeworth) and Portland Angel (Marcia Rodd – a natural comedienne of high calibre), a jock brother (Bruce McGill) who steals his gym-teacher's girlfriend (Candy Clark), and Hot Coffee (Aliz Elias), a plump, maternal hooker who Chrome Angel helps with the purchase of a motorhome so she can take her trade direct to the trucking fraternity.

These and several more cameos are full of a gentle humour, never exaggerated to parody and often fascinating in their interplay. There are some moments of near farce, though, such as the moment when Chrome Angel's two wives meet accidently on a bus, or the scene in which we see Spider's alcoholic father (Robert Blossom), who although they live together, refuses to talk to his son unless it's over the C.B.

But for all its beautifully studied, even poignant comedy, CITIZENS BAND flopped on its initial release, lacking the stars and therefore the promotional conviction of Paramount who whined, it is said, that audiences mistook the film's title for that of a musical! Their short-term solution was to butcher it, completely chopping the original ending which had Hot Coffee persuading the two Angel wives that one good husband between them was better than none at all, and re-titling it HANDLE WITH CARE. This alone immediately denied the film the attentions of the twenty or so million C.B. users that know the medium as a life-line or a rewarding communicator, the very people that the movie would've delighted. Rarely shown now, CITIZEND BAND shows, perhaps even more than MELVIN & HOWARD and FIGHTING MAD, Demme's fast-developing eye for the forgotten America that Hollywood barely acknowledges. At once improvisational and inspirational, it's a credit to all concerned.

USA	1977	95 mins.

Dir: Jonathan Demme *Prod:* n/a
Prod Co: n/a *Script:* Paul Brickman
Cast incl: Charles Napier, Paul Le Mat, Candy Clark, Marcia Rodd, Roberts Blossom, Ann Wedgeworth, Alix Elias, Bruce McGill and Ed Begley

---

CONVOY

Much as his JUNIOR BONNER offered an insight into the parochial world of professional rodeo, CONVOY finds Sam Peckinpah trying to use humour and cowboy romanticism to show us how things really are with truckers. He fails, however, because unlike BONNER, the essence of this film's plot is mobility, and he and scripter B.W.L. Norton are too busy keeping the show on the road to allow themselves the space to work on the nuance and incidentals. Without such documentary elements, CONVOY is a sketch rather than a portrait.

The plot, in itself, is quite improbable: Kris Kristofferson is Martin Penwald, or 'Rubber Duck' in the Citizens' Band nomenclature, adopted by the phalanx of truck drivers he leads in an all-purpose mercy dash/freedom odyssey through California and New Mexico. The procession starts after Penwald, Spider Mike and Love Machine are booked for speeding by a vindictive cop, 'Dirty' Lyle Wallace (Ernest Borgnine). Wallace takes a bribe to keep their names off the record, but high-tails after them when he hears them bad-mouthing him on the C.B. network. He catches them at a truckstop where a massive brawl ensues in which Wallace is injured. That's a signal for the trio to flee, taking a freelance photographer, Melissa (Ali McGraw) along with them in Penwald's cab. Wallace puts out a police alert, the trucking fraternity take note, and hence we have our CONVOY. After a lot of cartoon-comic stunts and a rather under-done sub-plot involving a vote-hungry senator who offers to champion the truckers' cause (which by then includes over-taxation, restrictive practices etc., etc.),

Spider Mike (Franklyn Ajaye) leaves the queue to visit his pregnant wife. Wallace somehow catches Mike, and jails him in a town called 'Truckers Hell' as bait for Penwald and his pals. They fall for it of course, but bulldoze the town to rubble with their trucks before rescuing the badly beaten Spider Mike. The furious Wallace places a troop of National Guardsmen at a bridge entrance, but Penwald drives straight at their ambush, his truck explodes in flames and falls into the drink. For those who live in fear of sequels, Penwald unfortunately survives.

Accompanying Kristofferson through most of this slapstick is Ms. McGraw but, except when she tries to gee-up t.v. crews covering the pow-wow between Governor Haskins and the truckers (rounded up on a campsite, just like a western wagon-train), her role is immaterial and her acting almost as granite-hewn as Kristofferson's. Their relationship is neither that of ardent lovers nor platonic, road-born mavericks – it just sort of sits there like a spare tyre, waiting to be used. In fact the only human sensitivity shown by Penwald is directed at a truckstop waitress and sometime lover (Cassie Yates). She surprises him on his birthday, which being a rough-tough sort of a guy, he'd forgotten, by gift-wrapping her naked form and sitting it in the back of his cab. This sad little gesture is the only time we're asked to consider the emotional deprivations of the men and women who work the highways, and Penwald cuts it short by matter-of-factly dumping the poor girl in favour of the woman Melissa (who just may be wealthy, of course).

The rest of the sentiments displayed in CONVOY are one's of male humour, camaraderie and doing What's Right – exactly the sort of stuff that passed for human sensitivity in all those Peckinpah-directed westerns. But here, anything remotely resembling subtlety is lost to a low-calorie script and stunts that make their own, simple language – Wallace's patrolcar careening through a religious billboard, a black lady driver running an all-white truck, and so on. The episode with Governor Haskins is under-utilised either as a dramatic interlude, or as a means of airing the real grievances that apparently make the truckers' lives so unbearable. (Needless to say, all the poor sods in this film still manage to buy the booze, gas and time they need for some endless, adolescent cake-walk through the American highway system).

In total, CONVOY misses its opportunities by miles, and although it may have done something to help Kristofferson's reputation at the box office, it didn't convince anyone he could act.

CONVOY   USA   1978
Dir: Sam Peckinpah   Prod: Robert M. Sherman
Prod. Co: EMI/United Artists   Script: B.W.L. Norton
Stunt Dir: Gary Combs
Cast incl: Martin Penwald (a/k/a/ Rubber Duck) – Kris Kristofferson;
           Melissa – Ali McGraw; 'Dirty' Lyle Wallace – Ernest
           Borgnine; Bobby 'Pig Pen' – Burt Young; 'Spider Mike' –
           Franklyn Ajaye; Governor Gerry Haskins – Seymour Cassel;
           Violet – Cassie Yates; Federal Agent Hamilton – Walter
           Kelley; co-starring: J.D. Kane, Billy E. Hughes, Whitey
           Hughes, Bill Foster, Thomas Huff, Larry Spaulding and Randy
           Brady

CORVETTE SUMMER (a/k/a The Hot One)

An odd choice for Mark Hammill after the success of STAR WARS, CORVETTE SUMMER ran into trouble even before it finished production – and didn't do much better afterwards. The early problems arose over the film's original title, STINGRAY, which was also the name of an indie production about to be picked up by Avco Embassy. A legal harangue ensued over who had the rights to the name besides

General Motors, with M-G-M the losers. They didn't have much to fight over, really, for CORVETTE SUMMER is a mediocre chase flic with only a juvenile twist: the quarry is Mark Hammill's customised Corvette, looking like something Corman rejected on grounds of tastelessness from DEATHRACE 2000, which gets stolen after months of painstaking student labour. Annie Potts adds a smidgen of humour and pathos as a naive, would-be hooker hyped up on the American deceit that the streets of Las Vegas are paved with gold... or at least rich tricks. But even the lightweight appeal of this starry-eyed, kinder-whore in her custom upholstered van rapidly diminishes when she succumbs to the idea of snaring Hammill, settling down and producing babies. Worse still, Hammill falls for this schtick himself even *before* he's got the motor back. The movie's climax is so laden with syrup, that it's a wonder it doesn't slide off the screen, and the routine car and bicycle (yes, bicycle) chases are executed with no more finesse than second rate t.v. detective mellers. This in itself is an indictment of scriptwriters Barwood and (director) Robbins, whose standards clearly dropped dramatically after the work they did on SUGARLAND EXPRESS.

USA	1978	94 mins.
Dir: Mathew Robbins		*Prod:* n/a
Prod. Co: M-G-M	*Script:* Hal Barwood and Robbins	

Cast incl: Mark Hammill, Annie Potts, Eugene Roche and Kim Milford

THE CROWD ROARS

First of the real road racing movies, THE CROWD ROARS provided yet another platform for the bravura misogyny of James Cagney and gave Howard Hawks a crack at capturing the excitement and noise (especially the noise) of the Grand Prix.

Cagney plays a cock-sure racing champ who disapproves of his younger brother's romance with Lee (Eric Linden and Ann Dvorak, respectively). Just to show him Real Men don't need women, Cagney ditches his own long-suffering paramour, Anne (Joan Blondell) and smacks Lee around a bit. The resultant family feud causes the death of Cagney's longtime racing pal, Spud Smith (Frank McHugh), which throws Cagney into a remorseful decline. Inevitably, there's a tear-jerking reunion with the two brothers and the Women Who Waited.

As in so many movies involving fast cars, THE CROWD ROARS lets the script take a back seat in favour of motorised thrills and spills. This prevented Kubec

Glasmon and John Bright, distinguished scriptwriters of their era, from exploring the mentality of a man who would cause such ructions in order to spare his sibling the unpleasant facts of life! Even the central romances aren't accorded the attention normally due the female leads of the 'twenties and 'thirties – a crying shame in the case of the doe-eyed Blondell. Cagney plays Cagney with his usual swagger, but even he needs a bit more tenable dialogue to wrap his bile around. That apart, Hawks, who was just starting to hit his stride at the time, does well with the action photography (given the technical limitations of the times) and the gung-ho atmosphere of vintage motor racing comes over convincingly. Why he didn't allow the scripters to make more of a story he originally wrote, is a mystery.

USA	1932	Length unknown
Dir: Howard Hawks		*Prod:* n/a
Prod. Co: Warner Bros.	*Script:* Kubec Glasmon and John Bright	

Cast incl: James Cagney, Joan Blondell, Ann Dvorak, Eric Linden, Guy Kibbee and Frank McHugh

CYCLE SAVAGES

Of those bike gang pics that actually do have storylines, CYCLE SAVAGES must surely be the most preposterous.

The curiously named Romko (Chris Robinson) plays a neatly groomed artist who, perhaps because he suffered excessive maternal attention during his childhood, loves sketching motorcycle gangs. His local neighbourhood gang leader, Keeg (Bruce Dern without a razor blade or shaving cream), takes exception to this. His best girl, Lea (Melody Patterson) doesn't. In fact, she doesn't to the point of posing nude for Romko in his spotlessly tidy little studio. When Keeg discovers this – and by now we've learnt that he is vaguely connected with a Las Vegas prostitution ring – he rounds up the boys and goes round to beat the crap out of Romko. Being handy with his fists (for an artist), Romko quickly recovers and beats the crap out of two of the gang. The requisite orgy scene follows, replete with Bacchanalian trappings of flying chicken breasts and bunches of grapes, which fires up Keeg and company with sufficient drunken angst that they go round and beat the crap out of Romko *again*. To add redundancy to injury, they crush the sensitive artist's hands in a vice. This act of sadism prompts Lea to capitulate to Romko's ardour in a display of hand-wringing condolence that only a biker girl is capable of mounting.

Dern would probably like to forget about CYCLE SAVAGES, as would its producer, currently the Lieutenant Governor of California, Mike Curb. (Curb and his company, Sidewalk Productions, were also responsible for numerous, and invariably atrocious, New World movie soundtracks. The unwholesome subjects of these matters would, it seems, have conflicted somewhat with his leadership of the Mike Curb Congregation, a mid-sixties pop group who were infamous for their anti-dope'n'sex crusade. California's a funny old place).

The sadistic exploits of Dern and his mob is the film's most abiding memory, although the forced juxtaposition of Romko's sensitive artistry and Keeg's malevolence won a place in my heart for director/writer, Bill Brame. I was also intrigued by the prospect of how far Dern could travel on a wheezing Triumph 650 with bits missing from its valve gear. That, and the fate of the buxom Melody Patterson who struggled womanfully to make something of her largely naked role, are answers lost in the oil mists of time.

USA	1970	80 mins (cut from 1982)
Dir: Bill Brame		*Prod:* Mike Curb
Prod. Co: Trans American Pictures		*Script:* Brame

Cast incl: Bruce Dern, Chris Robinson, Melody Patterson, Maray Ayres and Karen Ciral

DESPERATE

This is a nasty little story starring Raymond Burr – before he found fame in a wheelchair – as Radak, boss of a fur thieving gang, whose love for his younger brother, Al, prompts him to blackmail innocent truck driver Steve Randall (Steve Brodie) into taking the fall for the death of a nightwatchman: this being a crime that Al has been sentenced to death for. Randall manages to escape to the country with his young wife (Audrey Long), but they are trailed by Radak and his mob. After successfully evading the heavies, Randall throws himself at the mercy of the aptly named (for a road movie) detective, Ferrari, who reserves judgement on his guilt and uses him as a decoy to catch Radak.

Anthony Mann directs this competently scripted meller with considerable skill, making full use of the embryonic talents of the principal actors. Burr and Jason Robards, as Ferrari, are especially adept at milking as much tension as possible out of the chase, with Burr injecting a nice touch of indignant fury into many of his scenes. Brodie and Long are given to behaving like drippy newlyweds now and again, but Brodie's sense of righteous innocence is fairly convincing. Mann was already making a name for himself as a craftsman who never let pictorial bravura overwhelm his material. In the same year as he made DESPERATE, Mann completed one of his best-ever films T-MEN, but is best known for GOD'S LITTLE ACRE (1957), a benchmark western, THE MAN FROM LARAMIE (1955) and a couple of undercover-agent thrillers, REIGN OF TERROR and TALL TARGET (both 1951). All these were written by John Alton.

USA   1947   72 mins
Dir: Anthony Mann   *Prod. Co:* RKO Radio Pictures
Script: Harry Essex
Cast incl: Raymond Burr, Steve Brodie, Audrey Long, Jason Robards

DETOUR

"Nobody ever made good films faster, or for less money than Edgar Ulmer."
So wrote Peter Bogdanovitch in his introduction to a feature on the legendary B-movie
director in 'Film Culture' (1974). Ulmer had learnt his craft under Lang, working with
him as an assisstant on both METROPOLIS and SPIES before moving onto Universal and
directing silent westerns. Film-noir, however, is the genre most often associated with
Ulmer, his best remembered works being RUTHLESS, THE BLACK CAT and THAT
STRANGE WOMAN. DETOUR also fits loosely in that category, but in combining the
sinister and the mobile, Ulmer and his scriptwriter, Martin Goldsmith, created a road
movie that hovers tantalisingly between high camp and the grimmest sort of murder
thriller.

Down-and-out nightclub pianist Al Roberts (Tom Neal), decides to hitch
from New York to Los Angeles where his girlfriend, Sue (Claudie Drake) is a waitress.
He's picked up by a wealthy playboy, Charles Haskell, who becomes drowsy after
popping some pills, and asks Roberts to drive. Caught in a storm, Roberts hurriedly
tries to erect the coupé's rag-top and notices that Haskell has fallen into a coma. In the
ensuing struggle, Haskell falls out of the car, dead. Realising his predicament and not
wanting to face a murder rap, Roberts changes clothes with Haskell, takes his wallet,
and drives on. He then makes the mistake of giving a lift to Vera (Ann Savage), an
embittered tyro of a woman, who recognises the car and accuses Roberts of Haskell's
murder. She then blackmails him into handing over the money he's taken from Haskell,
which is but a short step from making him her virtual slave We then get to Hollywood,
Vera reads a newspaper report of the death of Haskell's father and orders Roberts to
impersonate his dead son and so claim the inheritance. Stricken with guilt, or so I'd
like to think, Vera starts hitting the bottle, gets her neck caught in the telephone cord
when she tries to shop Roberts to the police after he rebuffs her orders, and is
accidently strangled. Roberts then waits dejectedly to be arrested for the two
"murders" he didn't commit.

Compressed economically into 68 minutes, this nihilistic little story is acted
out with a kind of desperate aclarity by Neal and Savage. Vera's personality seems so
completely abandoned to evil and self-interest, it's hard not to admire her for having
the gall to be so unremittingly horrible; if you were to take her seriously, you'd be
utterly revulsed (and there's a direct parallel to Regina Baff's twisted whore in ROAD
MOVIE).

Ulmer pushes the story along with such manic zeal, that you soon ignore the
inconsistent back projection, Tom Neal's voice over links and all the other evidence of
an ultra low budget. DETOUR, although underrated, is certainly on a par with the
director's better known work.

USA	1945	68 mins

Dir: Edgar G. Ulmer   *Prod. Co:* P.R.C. Inc.
Script: Martin Goldsmith
Cast incl. Tom Neal, Ann Savage, Claudia Drake

THE DETOUR

At last – The Bulgarian road movie!

Not to be confused with the Edgar Ulmer classic reviewed above, this is a
lightweight but deliberately political example of European 'nouvelle vogue', although
'vague' might in fact be a more appropriate adjective.

Doctrinaire Marxist official, (Ivan Adenov), meets an old lover (Nevena
Kokanova) when he takes a detour en route to Sofia and passes the archeological site
where she works. In between the polite, solicitous conversation that their reunion

demands, they both silently reminisce about past loves. The flashbacks (with the actors convincingly made up to look twenty years younger than they are), emphasise the contrast between the idealistic optimism of their youth and the grey reality of depressed, post-war communism. After spending two weeks of dialectic debate and sometimes tender, romantic interludes together, the couple part company again and we are left with the rather sad conclusion that political will has triumphed over human spirit. A metaphor for latterday communism, in fact.

THE DETOUR is an evenly constructed film and the acting is as convincing as the sub-titles will permit, especially the lovers' final farewell. But the story is rooted in symbolism and political reference that is either too overstated or too remote to have any real veracity to western audiences. Director Grisha Ostrovski must, however, be admired for making a film so critical of his masters.

Bulgaria   1967   80 mins
Dir: Grisha Ostrovski   *Prod. Co:* Sofia Film Studios
Script: Blaga Dimitrova
Cast incl: Ivan Andenov, Nevena Kokanova

DEVIL'S ANGELS

And here we have Roger Corman exploiting Roger Corman, with a virtual re-make of his year-old WILD ANGELS. Unfortunately, Corman sits back as producer and lets a B-team take over; Dan Haller directing a script by redoubtable Corman ally, Charles Griffith, who also wrote WILD ANGELS. Between them they get the job done, but in a rather lacklustre style.

It is the story of the Skulls motorcycle gang and the mellowing of their leader, played by John Cassavetes with all the mumbling dissonance you'd expect of a committed method actor. Running from the cops after their involvement in a fatal bike accident, the Skulls pause briefly to liberate fellow outlaw Buck Kartalian from jail and, upon arriving at the small town of Brookeville, they terrorise a local beauty contest. Hopeful entrant (and ubiquitous outlaw biker moll) Mimsy Farmer, decides to join the gang for a beach party, soon realising her error of judgement when rape and brutality

48

threaten. The local sheriff pulls in Cassavetes, but dismisses Farmer's rape charge when she is revealed as an habitual liar. A sadder and wiser man, Cassavetes leaves town alone as another gang, the Stompers, arrive and begin a night of druggy frolic with the Skulls.

Not even engaging for its tackiness, DEVIL'S ANGELS represents an extraordinary career move by Cassavetes who'd just received excellent reviews for his performance in EDGE OF NIGHT, and was already recognised as a promising directorial talent. For Corman it represented just another participle of the Quick Buck ethic.

USA   1967   84 mins
Dir: Dan Haller   *Prod:* Roger Corman
Script: Charles B. Griffith
Cast incl: John Cassavetes, Mimsy Farmer, Beverly Adams, Leo Gordon

THE DEVIL'S HAIRPIN

This is a motor racing movie with Cornel Wilde directing himself in the role of Nick, a tyrannical ex-champ who almost kills his younger brother, Johnny (Larry Pennell). Wilde humiliates many of the ex-racers he's beaten by having them work as waiters in his restaurant, and generally toughs it up with anyone he comes into contact with. Then comes the Big Accident involving young Johnny, which prompts him to retire and search for forgiveness, which he certainly doesn't get from his mother (Mary Astor, with too much make-up). After his car is re-built by his raddled old mechanic (Paul Fix), Nick agrees to one more race and by showing uncharacteristic restraint during a dual on the Devil's Hairpin of the title, averts the death of old rival, Tony Botari (Morgan Jones), wins over his mum, and ex-girlfriend, Kelly (Jean Wallace), who swills martinis like a good 'un.

This obvious re-make of THE CROWD ROARS has only its technical superiority to commend it. Wilde over-acts and under-directs, and the rest of the cast are either dull or implausible. The action photography is okay, especially if you like the sexy shapes of 'fifties racing machinery.

USA   1957   83 mins
Dir: Cornel Wilde   *Prod:* Wilde
Prod. Co: Paramount   *Script.* James Edmiston & Wilde
Cast incl: Cornel Wilde, Jean Wallace, Mary Astor, Larry Pennell, Paul
                    Fix and Arthur Franz

DIRTY MARY CRAZY LARRY

Predating THE DRIVER by some four years, DIRTY MARY CRAZY LARRY is about another man who drives for ill-gotten gains. Fonda is an ex-stockcar racer (at least we know his background, Ryan O'Neal's DRIVER never even gave that much away), down on his beans and planning a $150,000 supermarket heist with his mechanic, Adam Roarke. Playing a feisty small town tart who sees the fleeing robbers as the wind of destiny that's going to spirit her away to better things, Susan George struggles with a Barbie Doll accent and lines even more prosaic than those of Fonda and Roarke. The story quickly degenerates into a frenetic chase with Vic Morrow hotly in pursuit as a helicopter-borne sheriff.

Stunt director Al Wyatt is really the star of this unevenly photographed jape, as he provides all there is to hold anyone's interest, the screenplay having long since abdicated any responsibility to establish the main characters. Fonda and George are merely crude stereotypes and the best attempt to bring any life into the dialogue comes from veteran exploitee, Roddy McDowall as the supermarket owner. Perhaps as a mark of self-respect, his name is absent from the credits.

DIRTY MARY CRAZY LARRY was at least energetically directed by John Hough, whose excellent LEGEND OF HELL HOUSE was completed immediately prior to this unfortunate turkey.

USA   1974   93 minutes
Dir: John Hough   *Prod:* Norman T. Herman
Prod. Co: 20th. Century-Fox   *Script:* Leigh Chapman, Antonio Santean
Cast incl: Peter Fonda, Susan George, Adam Roarke, Roddy McDowall,
Vic Morrow and Fred Daniels

DRIVE A CROOKED ROAD

The old story of the gangster's moll being forced to lure a worthy innocent into a life of crime which they both ultimately suffer for. Dianne Foster is the girl, Mickey Rooney is a luckless racing driver. He's been lined up by the mob to pilot the getaway car for a fast trip through the mountains, following a bank job in Palm Springs. Kevin McCarthy, as the gang's boss, doesn't realise that his girl Foster is falling hard for Rooney in the romance department until it's too late, and she's double-crossed him to try and save herself and her new-found beau from the law. Her ruse fails, McCarthy meets a violent end and Foster and Rooney meet the cops. The ending is a downer and the bank job that leads to it doesn't even get under way until the third reel. This leaves us with forty uneven minutes of racing and diverse other cinematic upholstery that only Mr. Rooney's most devoted fans will wish to endure. Richard Quine directs DRIVE A CROOKED ROAD with a sort of plodding efficiency, from one of Blake Edwards' earliest scripts.

USA   1954   83 mins
Dir: Richard Quine   *Prod:* Jonie Taps
Prod. Co: Columbia   *Script:* Blake Edwards
Cast incl: Mickey Rooney, Dianne Foster, Kevin McCarthy, Jack Kelly, Harry Landers and Paul Picerni

DRIVE HARD, DRIVE FAST

Fans of DYNASTY, BITCH and STUD will doubtless feel cheated that Joan Collins does not remove her clothes or drench anyone with verbal venom in DRIVE HARD, DRIVE FAST. She is, however, a scarlet woman, whose husband is on business in South America whilst she gets racing driver Brian Kelly to drive her to New Orleans... in her hubby's brand new sports car. Kelly notices another car following them at a discreet distance. The driver has planted a radio microphone in the couple's car and can hear every tedious word they're saying. Soon machete-wielding thugs are attacking people in motel rooms. Why? And do you care? Neither Kelly, Collins or anyone else in this Jo Swerling made-for-t.v. film do anything that commands our concern, so I advise you to change channels if it ever comes your way.

USA   1973   86 mins
Dir: Douglas Heyes   *Prod:* Jo Swerling Jr.
Prod. Co: MCA   *Script:* Matthew Howard
Cast incl: Brian Kelly, Joan Collins, Joseph Campanella, Henry Silva,
       Karen Huston and Frank Ramirez

DRAGSTRIP GIRL

Rubbish certainly, but camp rubbish and therefore quite fun to watch.

Fay Spain is the girl of the film's title and apart from hairspray, her main interests in life are boys and customised hot-rods. To satiate her fondness for the former, she has two men vying for her favours (i.e. a peck or two on the cheek). They are garage mechanic-cum-drag racer, Steve Terrell and playboy-cum-drag racer, John Ashley. Naturally Ashley is prevented from being anything other than a ne'erdowell by his very affluence, and to prove it he kills a hapless pedestrian during a high-speed zip through the city streets. Later on he loses the Big Race that the film builds clumsily up to, and Fay's favours to boot. Or rather to Terrell.

DRAGSTRIP GIRL was a prime example of big studio exploitation. You can almost hear Samuel Z. Arkoff yelling down to the front office, "Okay, you wanna make some money offa the hot-rod craze?" And then going off and producing his own, grossly distorted image of what it was all about and ensuring that everyone followed his party line; screenwriter, director and cast.

USA   1957   69 mins
Dir: Edward L. Cahn   *Prod:* Samuel Z. Arkoff & Alex Gordon
Prod. Co: Golden State   *Script:* Lou Rusoff
Cast incl: Fay Spain, Steve Terrell, John Ashley, Frank Gorshin, Russ
       Bender and Tommy Ivo

DRAGSTRIP RIOT

Another cash-in on the drag racing mini-trend, DRAGSTRIP RIOT threw in the dubious bonus of pop songstress Connie Stevens, warbling gooey ditties at the drop of a cheque.

Reformed teenage delinquent, Gary Clarke moves to Los Angeles with his ultra-strict parents, who somehow let him out of their sight long enough to fall in with a motor racing crowd. Winsome Yvonne Lime soon wins his heart, but true love runs anything but smoothly as she's already hitched to the rascally Bob Turnbull. By dint of obvious cheating, Bob dumps all over Rick in a drag race, is then challenged by the loser to a tricky stunt on a railroad track, whereupon he becomes the loser instead. To avenge his pride and show Janet what a man he is, Turnbull takes up with a cycle gang, one of whom Clarke has beaten-up in a past skirmish. (A movie with everything!) This engenders much highway violence, death and noisy activities in strange looking automobiles.

Although director/scriptwriter O. Dale Ireland threw in as many teen-inclined gimmicks as he could, DRAGSTRIP RIOT lacks one essential ingredient; melodramatic conviction. But, as I said of DRAGSTRIP GIRL, this doesn't stop it from being worth a look for a laugh.

USA   1958   68 mins
Dir: David Bradley   *Prod:* O. Dale Ireland
Script: George Hodgins & Ireland
Cast incl: Gary Clarke, Yvonne Lime, Bob Turnbull, Fay Wray, Connie
                Stevens, Gabe DeLutri and Ted Wedderspoon

THE DRIVER

Anyone baulking at glib analogies between road movies and the westerns of yore must surely yield to THE DRIVER. Plot, script and direction, all provided by Walter Hill, stand any comparison to spare, exquisitely violent, revenge-seeking oaters, particularly of the Clint Eastwood school and, indeed Hill's own under-praised classic, THE LONG RIDERS. As in the low-bucks spaghetti jobs, Hill's central character wades coldly, self-assuredly and anonymously through the action. And as if to emphasise the similarities, Hill even has his hero, played by Ryan O'Neal, referred to as "the cowboy", by his main adversary, Bruce Dern.

Thematic parallels are, however, merely an academic drum-roll to alert anyone who hasn't seen THE DRIVER to what is both a masterpiece of entertainment and a movie that approaches TWO LANE BLACKTOP, VANISHING POINT and ROAD MOVIE in its ability to reflect the driving experience as a way of life.

The story is a simple one. O'Neal is a top getaway driver with a frugal lifestyle and no apparent ambition other than to be the best there is. After a profitable casino heist, he tells his partners in crime that it's the last job he'll do with them, because they were a few *seconds* late running out of the joint. In those few seconds, Isabelle Adjani, playing a sullen faced gambler, makes eye contact with O'Neal but in the police line-up that follows, denies that he was at the scene of the crime. Dern is the detective in charge of this and other similar investigations, and vows to put The Driver of the film's title behind bars. Despite carping from his two deputies (Matt Clark and Felice Orlandi), Dern plans to snare O'Neal by setting him up in a fake bank raid. He blackmails a nervy, small-time stick up artist he's arrested (Joseph Walsh), into hiring O'Neal for a carefully staged hit on a bank he knows to be vulnerable. Although O'Neal wouldn't ordinarily touch a bunch of second-raters like Walsh and his gang, he senses Dern's involvement and can't resist the challenge. Adjani, meanwhile, busies herself by approaching O'Neal for hush-money after covering for him at the line-up. It seems she's a once-kept woman on the tail-end of sugar daddy's largesse, but O'Neal can hardly refuse her under the circumstances. The set-up is a failure, the bank-job turns into a homicidal disaster and O'Neal escapes with the money and the girl... or so it seems on the surface.

From the moment the titles are out of the way, the audience is left in little doubt that what we have here is a film about *serious* driving – a dynamite pursuit through downtown Los Angeles lasting a full five minutes and trashing as many police cars in the process. Everett Creach, the stuntman responsible for the chillingly precise carnage in THE LAST AMERICAN HERO and THE CAR quickly establishes O'Neal's cool confidence behind the wheel with sustained, carefully-paced footage that never once drifts into the dodgem-car vaudeville of lesser films. The audience is thrown into the back seat with the near-hysterical villains as O'Neal lurches and squeals down alley-ways and dimly-lit streets. In a later sequence Creach stretches credibility to rare limits, although only to those who know that the rear-end of a pick-up is just too skittish to out-run a 6.6 litre Trans-Am, even if it is driven by a stir-crazy young Mexican.

This is the first part of an epic chase which ends with a wonderfully off-beat game of hide and seek, driven at walking pace through the labyrinths of a crowded warehouse. Whether O'Neal is driving fast or slow, he maintains an impassive, unblinking facade, his only emotions expressed through quick shots of his feet stomping the pedals or his hands spinning the wheel, Philip Lathrop's action photography relies largely on available light, even though shot mostly at night, and the grainy, up-rated effects perfectly complement Creach's cunning stunt direction. Even though this isn't Cinerama, there are moments – such as the full-throttle descent down L.A.'s Ninth Street, or the head-on chicken run with two police cars – when there is considerable danger of cinema seat-wetting. And this moody, atmospheric "super-realism" wouldn't be nearly so effective were it not for the masterful continuity of its execution; it's as if these unusually long, five to fifteen minute excursions were completed in one take.

And if the driving sequences are handled with an impressive subtlety, the performances in THE DRIVER stand alongside those of LANE BLACKTOP as the epitome of restraint. Working from a script that couldn't have numbered more than a few dozen pages, Messrs. O'Neal, Dern and Adjani do little more than mumble or sneer monosyllabically at one another. This obviously appalled many of the film's critics, deterring them from any deeper analyses of either plot or characterisations, both of which have been dismissed as facile and one-dimensional. However, I find THE DRIVER an excellent, multi-lateral film about obsessions; Hill and the principal actors only tantalisingly hinting at the reasons behind these. In this respect, THE DRIVER is a demanding film to watch, but any work required of the audience is amply compensated for by its accessibility as a road movie.

The relationship between Adjani and O'Neal, for example, is clever exercise in innuendo. From the fleeting contact of their first meeting, there is a hint of kinship between these two outsiders. Not, you'll note, a bond between outlaws (c.f. EASY RIDER, THUNDERBOLT & LIGHTFOOT), but of urban, middle-class mis-fits who've somehow drifted into a lucrative, but unsavoury low-life. Hill's script makes this for a relationship which hovers ambiguously on the cusp of romance. We keep expecting, or at least hoping, that they'll suddenly drop their fortress-like guards and tear into a bout of carnal passion... but they never even kiss.

"You think maybe you can wait for a while," husks Adjani in the nearest they ever get to a clinch. And we're left guessing.

Less obfuscated is O'Neal's conflict with Bruce Dern. "I'm very good at what I do," he boasts to the driver. "I'm gonna catch the cowboy, the cowboy that's never been caught." And as he stands in O'Neal's seedy hotel room, and listens to the tinny country'n' western music on the radio, Dern extends the analogy: "Cowboy music. Always tells a story. Drunks, whores, broken hearts."

"I don't have any friends," O'Neal tells him, as if insulted that Dern could expect him to be like other, ultimately human criminal. And in that one short sentence, Hill's narrative lurches from patchy insinuation to an explicit admission of everything we've ever suspected as a motive for the wanderings and wrong-doings of a road movie hero; the man is lonely and, what's more, he wears his loneliness as some sort of badge of honour! And revealing though this may be, it's an admission calculated to enhance our sympathies for this numb, pragmatic villain.

It has no such effect on Dern, of course, who is by now on a trajectory of barely controlled mania. His career at risk if the set-up goes wrong, his subordinates questioning the morality of risking a bank's money on his personal vendetta and Walsh getting dangerously wobbly about the entire enterprise, the detective exhibits all your favourite Dern trademarks: bulging eyeballs; twitching cheeks and that laconic, "Well, well, well, lookie here" that announces every confrontation you can remember. The relatively short exchanges between Dern and his quarry confirms that Dern whilst gradually going off his rocker, is also rather in awe of the driver's resolve and skill. But is it merely this jealousy that lies behind his madness? Another conundrum.

Yes, THE DRIVER is chock full of unanswered questions, but for that very reason it is an absorbing, intelligent work and a blinder of a road movie. And even if you don't care for a film that is studded with such abstruse observations and conclusions, you can't deny that Ryan O'Neal plays an entirely different ball-game from that of PAPER MOON!

USA   1978   91 mins
Dir: Walter Hill   *Prod:* Lawrence Gordon
Prod. Co: 20th. Century-Fox/EMI   *Script:* Walter Hill
Photog: Philip Lathrop   *Stunt Dir:* Everett Creach
Cast incl: The Driver – Ryan O'Neal; The Detective – Bruce Dern; The Player – Isabel Adjani; The Connection – Ronee Blakley; Glasses – Joseph Walsh; co-starring Matt Clark, Felice Orlandi, Rudy Ramos, Denny Macko, Frank Bruno and Will Walker

DUEL

Originally filmed for television (see introduction), Steven Spielberg's first theatrical release sits alongside THE CAR as a film which successfully embraces both the horror and road movie genres. Indeed, DUEL goes one better than that by giving its audience a good scare, without relying on the contrivances that are invariably the resort of both types of cine-drama.

The film opens with salesman David Mann (Dennis Weaver) on his way to California. Irked by the heavy traffic on the freeway, Mann decides to take a minor road but soon finds himself frustrated by a smokey, road-hogging tanker which dangerously cuts him up after he has struggled to overtake it. Visibly fazed by this, he manages to pass the tanker again and stops at a garage where the mechanic warns him that he needs a new radiator hose. Whilst this exchange is going on, the tanker-truck stops too, its driver's face ominously hidden from Mann by the darkly tinted windscreen. After being admonished for some unstated misdemeanour during a telephone call to his wife, Mann sets off again, only to be unwillingly embroiled in a game of cat-and-mouse with the tanker. He's pushed into the path of oncoming traffic, forced to drive beyond the limits of his car and his ability, and thoroughly shaken all-round, before finally managing to find a truckstop where he can rest up. But there stands the truck, almost glowering at him with contempt, and Mann decides there and then to apprehend its driver. Unfortunately he picks on the wrong man and gets into a fight, and when he manages to extricate himself from this embarrassing situation, the truck has left. But Mann is soon set upon again, the truck becoming more and more reckless as it pushes him onto a level crossing just as a train is bearing down. By now thoroughly terrified, Mann finds a phone booth adjacent to a roadside snake farm, and is about to call the police when the truck suddenly appears and trashes the snake cages *and* the phone booth. Realising that the truck is on some sort of homicidal mission, Mann tries to lose it in a quarry, but his radiator hose bursts and he's obliged to jump out and make a run for it as the tanker speeds towards him. The film ends as Mann looks on with disbelief whilst the truck takes his car over the edge of a precipice in a ball of flame.

DUEL is a delicately choreographed confrontation between well defined American stereotypes; a reasonably-minded middle class executive in his reasonable, middle-class Plymouth Valiant, versus an envoy from a familiar, but somehow closed order, that of the trucking fraternity. These are the prejudices and the images that Richard Matheson's script articulates so insidiously. Matheson, who wrote both story and screenplay, collaborated on some of Roger Corman's early gothic horror movies and is no stranger to the extraction of human fear. By the time Mann has arrived at the snake farm for example, Matheson aggravates our already considerable phobia of the menacing truck, by unleashing a quick splurge of reptilian paranoia! In both cases Matheson bludgeons us, but in a fairly tasteful manner, with the threat of the unknown amidst the extremely familiar.

Other directors working with small budgets have used this same premise to good effect – John Carpenter with HALLOWEEN and Alfred Sole with COMMUNION, for example – but with DUEL Spielberg had to overcome two problems peculiar to the genre. Firstly, the very threat of the truck could only be established by shooting extremely long takes requiring split-second timing and precise photographic continuity. Secondly, a lone driver such as DUEL's David Mann doesn't even have an in-car dialogue to help him express his reactions to the dangers of the chase.

Spielberg's technique of story-boarding the action sequences and shooting in continuity were touched on in my introduction, and his considerable admiration for stunt co-ordinator Cary Loftin explains much of his success in shooting the mobile battle between truck and car. As for the fact of Mann's isolation, Spielberg skirted the problem by having Dennis Weaver record his thoughts and reactions over each day's rushes. It would've been impractical to stick a microphone and a mixing engineer in the car with the noise of the action going on all around him, and in any case, the idea of Mann literally talking to himself strained the credibility of the script. The result was a monologue of fractured, mounting hysteria that remained completely faithful to what

was happening on the screen. It effectively built up a picture of a timorous, unconfident little man pursued by an unknown force — a metaphor for the uncertainties of his own life.

And from the incidental information provided by the storyline – Mann's discord with his wife, the irritatingly mindless pap on his car radio, the broken hose on his brand new car – we begin to appreciate that the fabric of David Mann's comfortable middle-class life is already showing signs of wear. Can it sustain the unrelieved emotional attrition of his battle with the truck? That's a question lodged somewhere in the back of our minds as DUEL unfolds. Clever and subtle though this is, it lacks the resolution of films like THE CAR, or Hitchcock's THE BIRDS because Matheson's screenplay offers us no conclusion whatsoever, whereas the other two essays on mysterious menace at least suggest that there is more to come. Mann's ordeal is over when the tanker explodes at the bottom of a ravine, but where does that leave him? Or us?

USA   1972   90 mins.
Dir: Steven Spielberg   *Prod:* George Eckstein
Prod. Co: Universal   *Script:* Richard Matheson
Photog: Jack A. Marta   *Stunt Dir:* Cary Loftin
Cast incl: David Mann – Dennis Weaver; Mrs. Mann – Jacqueline Scott;
           Cafe Owner – Eddie Firestone; Lady at Snakerama – Lucille
           Benson; also featuring Shirley O'Hara, Charles Seel, Alexan-
           dra Lockwood, Amy Douglass and Dale Van Sickle

EAT MY DUST

Almost a decade after he scripted THE WILD ANGELS and BORN LOSERS, Charles Griffith gets to sit in the director's chair as well as behind the typewriter, with EAT MY DUST. The dual responsibility appears to have been a bit too much for him, I'm afraid.

High school grad and auto racing fan Hoover Niebold (Rod Howard) highjacks the winning car in a local race to prove his general all-round butchness to teenage vamp, Darlene (Christopher Norris, who is either a carelessly named girl or a very convincing transvestite). The remainder of this 89 minute film is simply an excuse for Niebold, Darlene and assorted college chums to tear round the countryside, pursued by cops and making trouble. The local sheriff just happens to be Niebold's dad, and he throws anyone who protests about his son's activities into jail. Pro race drivers join the chase and Darlene eventually ditches her would-be suitor after a highly metallic climax.

EAT MY DUST is a silly story devoid of characterisation and containing only the skimpiest attempt at the sort of satirical humour the endless stunts seem to beg for. Only Warren Kemmerling as Niebold's drunken father distinguishes himself in the acting department and Griffith's direction is just slightly more lively than his script... but for "lively" you could also read "wilfully erratic". This type of cartoon-slapstick chase movie needs a greater percentage of conscious fun in it to work properly. But since Griffith began his career working on a string of Corman gore-mongers like BUCKET OF BLOOD and LITTLE SHOP OF HORRORS, maybe he just doesn't have a sense of humour.

USA   1976   89 mins.
Dir: Charles B. Griffith   *Prod:* Roger Corman
Prod Co: New World   *Script:* Griffith
Cast incl: Ron Howard, Christopher Norris, Warren Kemmerling, Dave
           Madden, Evelyn Russel and Charles Howerton

EASY RIDER

EASY RIDER's story is by now as well known as its title, for here is a film that became a symbol and even a metaphor for its generation.

Two drifters, Wyatt (a/k/a Captain America) and Billy, (Peter Fonda and Dennis Hopper, who also directed), complete a large coke deal, the proceeds of which will buy them the freedom to do what they want for a while. And what they want to do is drive two Harley-Davidson choppers down to New Orleans for Mardi Gras. En route from Los Angeles, they are fed by Mexican-American homesteaders, who seem to raise children as prolifically as crops and pick up a hippy boy who takes them to his impoverished farming commune, where Wyatt and Billy frolic with a couple of the female incumbents. Later on, they are arrested for upsetting a carnival parade and thrown into a small-town jail where they meet George Hanson (Jack Nicholson), an alcholic lawyer who's sleeping off his hangover. After springing them from jail, Nicholson elects to join them on their journey to New Orleans, but after a brutal encounter with southern red-necks, is beaten to death in his sleeping bag. Shocked, but motivated by their own safety, Wyatt and Billy continue to New Orleans where they fulfill Hanson's dream of visiting a gaudy whorehouse. They entice two of the hookers, Mary (Toni Basil) and Karen (Karen Marmer) to join them in some LSD and a swing through the Mardi Gras parade. This ends in a blaze of 16mm cinema verité in a baroque cemetery.

After they finally leave New Orleans, the two men are taunted by a pair of red-necks in a pick-up truck. Billy's defiant response leading to their immediate and bloody death.

Dennis Hopper has admitted that EASY RIDER was a self-conscious reflection of America's decaying moral imperatives: "At the start of the movie, Peter and I do a very American thing – we commit a crime, we go for the easy money. We go for the easy money and then we're free. That's one of the big problems with the country; everybody's going for the easy money. I think Americans basically feel the criminal way is all right *if you don't get caught;* crime pays *if* you get away with it."

And Hopper's film attacks social duplicity on many levels: the good, God-fearing burghers who disparage Hanson, Billy and Wyatt in a coffee shop with talk of faggotry and cowardice, then sneak up while they're sleeping and beat them with axe-handles; the background dialogue between two commune girls who complain that recent visitors refused to hand over any of their dope, in the same breath defending their refusal to give the same visitors some of their flour; Wyatt assuring the sceptical Billy that the commune farmers are going to nurture a crop from their barren land, without offering them either help or any of the $10,000 they've got stashed in their gas-tanks; the cops who bust Billy and Wyatt for playfully joining their town parade, but respectfully shield Hanson's drinking problem from his moneyed family.

Yet despite this increasingly dismal picture of middle-American malaise, Hopper and his cameraman, Laszlo Kovaks, present an affectionate, even reverential view of the American landscape. Hanging together scenes of violence and degradation are massive contrasts of travel footage... Billy and Wyatt ride along, pointing out the scenery to each other in childish wonderment... deserted backroads disappear into breathtaking mountain vistas... sunsets drench the desert with an intoxicating beauty. This prepares us for another statement of paradox, as after the two men engage in a stoned campfire conversation about past cultures and their respect for the land, they awake amidst a detritus of abandoned tract housing and its attendant garbage.

As with its visual metaphors, EASY RIDER's script, written by Fonda and Hopper with assistance from Terry Southern, is spartan and tends to deny the characters any of the substance they mourn the lack of in the rest of the human race. Fonda and Hopper talk in infuriatingly trite hippy jargon, "Hey man," "Dig it," and

"That's cool," bluntly obstructing any meaningful utterance they might be trying to come out with. Only Nicholson's George Hanson is at all articulate, and paradoxically enough, he's a two-bit lawyer whose refuge is the bourbon bottle rather than a grass joint. According to Hopper, the contrast was deliberate:

"You run into Jack Nicholson and the whole picture changes. He's the only one constructed to be three-dimensional, and the only character whose background and present situation are developed. You're told a lot about Jack: his father's powerful, he played football in school, he's a lawyer for the American Civil Liberties Union, he's poisoning himself with alcohol, he sees flying saucers. You learn an awful lot about him. Jack *is* America: he's Trapped America, killing himself. As far as the other people go, you just don't know much about them, just basics.

"You get no background on the two hookers. You don't know what the commune is really into. Obviously I wanted to get closest to Jack. All you know about Captain America and Billy is that they sell cocaine, smoke grass, ride bikes. You don't know that they were trick bike riders who worked travelling carnival shows, rodeo, and so on. You don't know that Captain America and Billy originally made their living jumping bikes through flames, etc. At one time, this rodeo stuff was the first scene in the movie. But I finally decided not to do it that way. To explain all that is disturbing to me. You see, in the kind of t.v. shows and movies I've done for the past fifteen years, everything's explained. I mean *everything*. I mean: if some kid has ten lines, you know who his father, mother, uncle, brother are; and you know his dog died when he was three and that's why he's a racing driver. Right? Now I'm no longer interested in telling you all that. I hope that if you just *watch* the characters, you can understand all you need."

But if George Hanson says more about the in-bred hyprocrisies of his society in one monologue that Billy and Wyatt manage to mumble in the whole film, it remains a measure of EASY RIDER's realism that their language and mildly hedonistic behaviour faithfully reflects the times they lived in. In fact one of the film's drawbacks is that it's aged so badly. The soundtrack music, contemporary rock songs which seemed so bold and so right at the time, now seem forced and embarrassing. The acid-trip sequence, shot on 16mm and blown to distort both colour and texture, also looks anachronistic and self-conscious when viewed in the 'eighties.

"Some of that footage had stains on it," recalls Hopper, "but those were stains that came on the film. And one day it was raining, and another day not – so, different light. But I believe what Cocteau said: 'Ninety per cent of all creation is accident, one per cent logic.' I believe that; you must keep *free* for things to happen, for the accident – and then learn how to use the accident. It was a mess at Mardi Gras. I took over the camera myself at one point. Fifteen men threatened to walk out. There was this great question whether I would go on directing the movie after that. Nobody understood what the hell I'd shot in 16mm. Everybody was asking, 'Well, what is the acid trip sequence like?' So I held back from editing the footage until the last, saying, 'Nobody'll be able to unravel this part of the film but me, so they can't finish the film without me.' We shot as much film at Mardi Gras as we shot for the rest of the movie").

Technically the film is both flawed and inspirational. Kovak's camerawork is generally lyrical, sometimes too much so for its own good, in fact, and a number of the set-ups are just terrific; Phil Spector as the coke dealer, conducting business at the end of Los Angeles' airport runway whilst jets scream a few feet over their heads, the gaudy discomfort of the New Orlean brothel are two examples. Yet the graveyard acid trip, with Fonda wrapped around a marble madonna screaming hatred for his mother, is just slovenly and crass. Hopper's editing techniques, learnt from his years in television, were anything but crude however, especially his trick of breaching the gap between scenes by flashing in frames from a future set-up into the tail-end of the one that preceded it.

As he explains: "The light-energy bouncing on the screen like that, the six frame hypnotic flash hitting you, pushing you into the next scene is better, much better than dissolving one image over into another – that's terribly romantic and sentimental to me. And I think that now's not a time for that... we don't have time for that now. This is a problem of me controlling myself. Originally I had a lot of flash-forwards all through this film. For example, in an earlier version, on that first morning when Peter looks up at the sun flaring through the rafters, I had him flash-forward to a lot of things: Mardi Gras, Jack Nicholson, the stranger on the road, the commune. Very abstract, quick flashes. Finally I cut this down to just one flash; his death flash in the whore-house.

"We had the same film all along, but in different versions; 240-minute, 220-minute, 180-minute, 160-minute, and finally 94-minute. Basically it was my discipline problem. I loved the 220-minute version because you got the real feeling for the Ride – very hypnotic, very beautiful, like in 2001. One of the things I liked in 2001 was the hypnotic feeling of movement. We had that at one time with the bikes. You really felt like you crossed country with the bikes. But how many people were going to sit through three hours and forty minutes of bike riding and dig it? So it came down to the fact that I wanted to communicate... to reach as many people as possible. And I decided a 94-minute verson would do that best."

USA   1969   94 mins.
Dir: Dennis Hopper   *Prod:* Bert Schneider
Prod. Co: Pando Prods. *Script:* Hopper, Peter Fonda and Terry Southern.
Photog: Laszlo Kovaks
Cast incl: Wyatt – Peter Fonda; Billy – Dennis Hopper; George Hanson –
          Jack Nicholson; Lisa – Luana Anders; Sarah – Sabrina Scharf;
          Mary – Toni Basil; Karen – Karen Marmer; Connection – Phil
          Spector; also featuring: Arnold Hess Jnr., Keith Green, Sandly
          Wyeth, Robert Ball, Luke Askew, Cathi Cozzi and George
          Fowler Jnr.
          Quotes taken from an interview with L.M. Kit Carson in
          'Atlantic Review'.

ELECTRA GLIDE IN BLUE

ELECTRA GLIDE IN BLUE's director, James William Guercio, was previously manager, producer and sometime songwriter for early 'seventies mega-band, Chicago. And just so's you can't ignore the fact, he tacked seven minutes of Chicago playing one of his songs, "Tell Me", onto the end of the film.

But by then, the audience might've expected this sort of random posturing, for unexplained scenes and dialogue abound throughout this, his first film. Which is a shame, for ELECTRA GLIDE has a lot of promise shuffled between the obscure camera angles and disparate, often irrelevant scenes. Like EASY RIDER whose ending it plagiarises in a nicely twisted way, the film is a chronicle of disillusion. John Wintergreen (Robert Blake) is a pint-sized motorcycle patrolman who wins the promotion he craves by correctly figuring out that a suspected suicide was in fact a murder. But elevated to four wheels as the Chief of Detective's (Mitchell Ryan) driver, he is dismayed to find that his boss is sadistic, sexually deviant and *extremely* paranoid. Foolishly voicing his distaste for the Chief's behaviour, Wintergreen is soon back on his Harley-Davidson, dreams of fast girls and fast action shattered for ever.

Robert Blake brings a touching humanity to the cop who naively assumed that honesty and success are compatible. And when the photography isn't wallowing in symbolism, and Chicago's soundtrack isn't deafening its audience, ELECTRA GLIDE IN BLUE is a charming little movie trying to be something bigger, rather like its hero.

USA   1973   95 mins.
Dir: James William Guercio   *Prod:* Guercio
Script: n/a
Cast incl: Robert Blake, Mitchell Ryan, Jeannine Riley and Billy Green
         Bush

FEVER HEAT (a/k/a Stockcar)

This started out as a 109 minute meller wherein retired stockcar racer, Nick Adams was encouraged to return to the fray by his deceased racing buddy's widow and the staff of a small-town garage she owns. It was then called STOCKCAR and pandered to the legion of enthusiasts who patronised the clay ovals of the mid-west, by packing its convoluted and one-dimensional story with huge dollops of racing footage.

Re-edited and severely truncated for European markets as FEVER HEAT, Russell Doughten's film becomes almost incomprehensible and bereft of much of the so-so action photography that at least offered something to racing fanatics. Leaden acting and clumsy editing only weaken what was already an easily ignored production.

USA	1968	80 mins. (cut from 109)

Dir: Russell S. Doughten Jnr.   *Prod:* Doughten
Prod. Co: Heartland Prods.   *Script:* Henry Gregor Felsen
Cast incl: Nick Adams, Jeannine Riley, Norman Alden, Vaughn Taylor, Daxson Thomas and Robert Broyles

THE GAUNTLET

THUNDERBOLT & LIGHTFOOT was his first road movie as an actor, but in his second, THE GAUNTLET, Clint Eastwood successfully wills himself even further out of his Man With No Name and Dirty Harry persona by giving himself the useful perspective of the director. And, perhaps unsurprisingly, he does it by combining a clever mixture of the vigilante cowboy's cynical angst, and the urban cunning of his gun-happy detectives.

But to start with, Eastwood's Ben Shockley is a drunken, down-sliding cop, despatched from Phoenix, Arizona to bring in an important corruption trial witness from a Las Vegas jail. Despite the name, Gus Malley turns out to be a woman (Sondra Locke), and angrily warns Shockley that someone will try and kill her if she leaves her cell. His scepticism at this quickly dissolves when the ambulance he smuggles her out in is ambushed on the way to the airport, but by dint of supreme heroics, they manage to escape to Malley's house. Raddled by the distinctly homicidal nature of his assignment, Shockley phones his boss, Chief Blakelock (William Prince) and is assured that help is on the way. What arrives instead is a posse of police sharp-shooters who literally demolish the house with their gun-fire. The couple manage to flee down a sewer and abduct a patrolman who knowingly warns them that they're now on the run from the Mafia as well as the police. Malley, however, refuses to tell Shockley why this might be. After a further police ambush on the state line, and being chased by a helicopter on the Harley that Shockley takes from a biker gang, the pair rest up in a motel room. Here they capitulate to lust and troth-plighting – they're both a couple of softies underneath it all – and make plans to make it back to Phoenix and expose Blakelock for the criminal that Shockley now knows he is.

This requires them to commandeer a bus, reinforce the driving area with thick steel plate, and drive into town expecting the massed firepower of the Arizona State Police. In a last ditch attempt to save his corrupt skin, Blakelock uses an old colleague of Shockley's as a decoy, but the man is shot before our hero's very eyes, and the bus goes on to its appointment with bullet-splattered destiny. But you know who gets the final shot.

THE GAUNTLET is a solid, workman-like thriller that allows Eastwood to indulge his sardonic humour and macho resolve in equal measure, but without letting the whole thing depend on it. The story is almost credible, and in the role of the unwilling victim, Sondra Locke is a perfect little vixen, always spouting tart homilies to chide or admonish Eastwood's too-honest cop. "The only difference between a whore and a cop," she snarls at him during one particularly lively exchange, "is that a cop can't wash his sins off in the bath."

Only the gratuitous use of guns really lets the film down, for by the time the bus-cum-tank is finally struggling to the steps of City Hall, the audience is so bullet-drunk that the film's parable of corruption in high places doesn't seem as morally shocking as it's surely supposed to.

USA	1977	109 mins.

Dir: Clint Eastwood   *Prod:* Robert Daly

Prod. Co: Malpaso   *Script:* Michael Butler and Dennis Shyrack
Cast Incl: Clint Eastwood, Sondra Locke, William Prince, Michael Cavanaugh, Pat Hingle, Bill McKinney and Carver Barnes

THE GETAWAY

Just sneaking into this book by a hairsbreadth, THE GETAWAY qualifies as a road movie because slightly over half the story takes place on the move, and some of the best dialogue and plot exposition unfolds inside cars.

The film opens with Doc McCoy (Steve McQueen) in a Texas jail, plotting a parole scam which seems to involve his wife, Carol (Ali MacGraw) sleeping with a prison board official, Jack Benyon (Ben Johnson) and giving him half the take in a proposed bank heist. In the getaway following the bank job, the McCoys find themselves alternatively chasing and being chased by their vicious accomplice, Rudy Butler (Al Lettieri) who tries to abscond with the loot which they then retrieve. Their violent clashes give director Sam Peckinpah plenty of scope to deploy the exploding blood capsules and slow-motion camera-work that is as predictable as Walter Hill's script. But there's a steady tension throughout the film, fuelled as much as anything else by McQueen patiently waiting until they've got safely away before punishing his wife for her stupidity and/or infidelity. The scene in which he finally slaps her around caused feminists to flinch when it was first released, but far more sadistic was the relationship between Butler and a rural veterinary surgeon he staggers to when badly wounded. The vet (Jack Donaldson) is a wimpish little man with a bored, promiscuous wife, (Sally Struthers), and Butler kidnaps him as his driver, ties him to a chair and forces him to watch as he screws his wife in motel bedrooms.

Shot entirely on location and in continuity in Texas, THE GETAWAY also boasts some fine driving footage, especially when Ali MacGraw becomes the first lady of road movies in a snazzy display of evasive driving. Not up to the standard of then hubby McQueen in BULLITT, perhaps, but at least there's more of it!

USA   1972   122 mins.
Dir: Sam Peckinpah   *Prod:* David Foster and Mitchell Brower
Prod Co: First Artists   *Script:* Walter Hill
Cast Incl: Steve McQueen, Ali MacGraw, Al Lettieri, Ben Johnson, Slim Pickens, Sally Struthers, Jack Dodson and Richard Bright

GIRL ON A MOTORCYCLE

GIRL ON A MOTORCYCLE is a very silly film which sets out to establish the sexual symbolism of motorcycles by having its heroine Rebecca (Marianne Faithful), recite hilarious lines like, "My black motorcycle devil makes love beautifully..." as if we (and presumably the motorcycle) are supposed to take it seriously.

Married just two months she is already bored with her safe, respectable husband (Roger Mutton), and decides to visit her ex-lover, Daniel (Alain Delon, seen only in flashback), on the gleaming Harley-Davidson that he gave her as a wedding present, (surely hubby must've been a bit suspicious about *that*?). As she rides through the back-projection toward Heidelberg where he awaits her, Rebecca relives their past amour together and her eventual marriage to a stupid schoolteacher. The throb of the motorcycle greatly enhances the more sensuous aspects of all this, of course.

Director Jack Cardiff takes every opportunity to assail us with titillating shots of Marianne in and out of her fur-lined, black leather jumpsuit, plus lots of Vaseline-edged panoramas of pastoral France. This may pre-date David Hamilton and the sort of limp-porn that nice young couples can safely watch in suburban cinemas, but it also makes for a damn boring road movie.

Great Britain/France   1968   91 mins.
Dir: Jack Cardiff   *Prod:* William Sassoon
Prod. Co: Mid-Atlantic/Ares   *Script:* Ronald Duncan
Cast incl: Marianne Faithful, Roger Mutton, Alain Delon, Marius Goring, Catherine Jourdan and Jean Leduc

GRAND PRIX

Of all the films that employ auto racing as their raison d'etre, GRAND PRIX ranks alongside LE MANS as the films that most effectively capture the excitement and kinetic energy in purely visual terms. In GRAND PRIX, director John Frankenheimer's avowed fascination for technology is ornamented by "visual consultant" Saul Bass, who created split– and multi-screen techniques which articulate the progress of the cars in a far more lucid manner than snatched shots on corners or follow-on footage from a pace car.

Originally presented in Cinerama, some of the individual racing vistas do, however, stun the senses, especially a multi-camera shot of two colliding cars, one jettisoning into Monte Carlo harbour, the other disintegrating on a cliff. Unfortunately Frankenheimer has succumbed to that fatal mistake duscussed in my introduction: his script, by Robert Allan Arthur, is no more than a shaggy weave of basically dull characters who meander through the motor racing circus. The cast includes James Garner, Eve Marie Saint, Yves Montand and Toshiro Mifune, reflecting a chic, cosmopolitan society alright, but failing to ginger what is little more than a glum exercise in romantic intrigue barely worthy of a t.v. soaper. Stretched across 169 minutes (cut from 179!), the screenplay's frailty is all too obvious, and the initial impact of the action photography and special effects fail to compensate beyond the first two reels. Sheer stamina and race car lust required for this one.

USA   1966   169 mins.
Dir: John Frankenheimer   *Prod:* Edward Lewis
Pro. Co: Joel/JFP/Cherokee   *Script:* Robert Alan Arthur
Cast incl: James Garner, Eva Marie Saint, Brian Bedford, Yves Montand,
Toshiro Mifune, Françoise Hardy and Adolfo Celi

GRAND THEFT AUTO

A film for which the term "screwball comedy" was clearly coined, GRAND THEFT AUTO follows the pursuit of eloping teenies, Sam Freeman and Paula Powers (Ron Howard and Nancy Morgan) from L.A. to Las Vegas, by Paula's father (Barry Cahill). The film is noteworthy for several reasons:

It holds the record for the most set-ups in one day – ninety one which is altogether nine more than the previous record, (naturally accorded to another New World production, HOLLYWOOD BOULEVARD). It was also the first attempt by its star, Ron Howard, at directing and, betraying a nepotism blatant even by Hollywood standards, features both his father and younger brother in the cast.

Given that he really only had to oversee stunt co-ordinator Victor Rivers organise a succession of car crashes, Howard directs this mindless romp as competently as he acts in it. And as an actor he had plenty of experience, having started out in AMERICAN GRAFFITI, moved onto a regular role in t.v.'s HAPPY DAYS, which he took time out from to make GRAND THEFT, taking Marion Ross with him to play the mother of Paula's idiot fiancée. Corman regulars Don Steel and Joe Dante also helped keep things cosily familiar.

USA   1977   89 mins.
Dir: Ron Howard   *Prod:* Jon Davison
Prod. Co: New World   *Script:* Ranse and Ron Howard
Cast incl: Ron Howard, Nancy Morgan, Marion Ross, Ranse Howard,
Barry Cahill, Pete Isacksen, Don Steele and Hoke Howell

THE GRAPES OF WRATH

In its day, THE GRAPES OF WRATH was hailed as *the* greatest film ever made, and even now it stands as a masterpiece of American cinema along with CITIZEN KANE and EAST OF EDEN. Its greatness lies almost equally in its acting, script, photography and direction, but the film's original impact stemmed as much from its subject matter, for GRAPES OF WRATH was a caustic indictment of government failure.

Specifically, John Ford took Nunnally Johnson's sympathetic adaption of Steinbeck's classic novel of dustbowl depression and made it come alive. Johnson had rightly concentrated on Steinbeck's characters, escaped convict Tom Toad (Henry Fonda) and his family, buckling under the weight of poverty and finally humiliated into vagrancy by eviction from their homestead. In Fonda's strained dignity and occasionally unleashed anger, in his wife's (Jane Darwell) anguished break with her past, and in Casy's (John Carradine) pragmatic efforts to benefit his fellow men by turning from the church to union organisation, THE GRAPES OF WRATH shows us the nature of broken spirit and also the self-healing properties of hope.

Ford was never a man to mine the inner emotions of his actors, but the material and the manpower he was working with in GRAPES clearly got the better of him. Fonda delivers the performance of his life and Carradine also provides something for his off-spring to aspire to: watch Fonda switch from the necessary violence of a cop-killing to the mortal fear of being caught and again incarcerated for his crime, or Carradine exhorting the exploited crop-pickers into politicising their last shreds of dignity... brilliant and often moving stuff.

But Ford's talent was in catalysing the elements essential to what was obviously sociological dynamite in 1940 when the government of the day clearly could, or would not control the collapse of America's economy. Perhaps his best ally was photographer, the legendary Gregg Toland, whose sweeping panoramas of the dustbowl road-scape have a kind of bleak grandeur to them which is as affecting as any verbal statement contained in the script. (This aspect of GRAPES was not lost on Peter Bogdanovitch who clearly went for it in PAPER MOON, and possibly Wim Wenders too, with his KINGS OF THE ROAD, both of which were rather gratuitously shot in monochrome).

Ford and Toland were alleged to have shot a lot more "road" footage and several complete theatrical scenes along the Route 66 which was the standard migratory route of the dispossessed. Including this in greater measure might've relieved the principals of the burden of establishing the nature of the times to quite the extent they bear it, and also given GRAPES a little more of the pace of a classic road-movie. But if you weren't aware of the un-used film stock, and you weren't writing a book on road movies, you certainly wouldn't mourn its scarcity.

USA   1940   128 mins.
Dir: John Ford   *Prod:* Darryl F. Zanuck
Prod. Co: 20th Century Fox   *Script:* Nunnally Johnson
Cast incl: Henry Fonda, John Carradine, Jane Darwell, Charley Grapewin, Dorris Bowden, Russell Simpson, Frank Darien, O.Z. Whitehead and Zeffie Tilbury

THE GUMBALL RALLY

Yet another working of the coast-to-coast road race formula with jokes, zany characters and sub-plots all aimed firmly at the tiny-tots market Walt Disney carved out with HERBIE. House-wives paying for car repairs with sex and bouts of fisticuffs with some Hell's Angels, rather upset Warner Brothers' plans in this respect, for THE GUMBALL RALLY garnered an A-certificate in Britain. This means that I can't even recommend the film as a useful device for getting rid of the kids during school hols!

USA   1976   106 mins
Dir: Chuck Bail   *Prod:* Bail
Prod. Co: First Artists/Warner Bros.   *Script:* Leon Capetanos
Cast incl: Michael Sarrazin, Normann Burton, Raul Julia, Gary Busey,
Susan Flannery, Tricia O'Neil and Joanne Nail

THE HARD RIDE

Producer/director/writer Burt Topper tries to do a Corman and fails. THE HARD RIDE has an inane script existing mainly on the premise that even outlaw bikers should respect dead Vietnam veterans, the acting is just about up to high school standards and the direction, moribund. Robert Fuller plays the chap charged with honouring his dead buddy's death and making damn sure that all his other biking buddies turn up at the chapel for the service. The rest of it is too dumb to go into here. Possibly the worst film ever made, certainly the worst soundtrack album.

USA   1970   90 mins
Dir: Burt Topper   *Prod:* Topper
Prod. Co: Burwalt Prods   *Script:* Topper
Cast incl: Robert Fuller, Sherry Bain, Tony Russel, William Bonner,
Marshall Reed, Mikel Angel, Biff Elliot and Al Cole

HELL DRIVERS

Just about the best thing going for HELL DRIVERS is its cast – a veritable nursery of British cinema talent fascinating to watch as they all try furiously to out-act each other. Stanley Baker (before toupee), plays Tom Yately, ex-prisoner who takes a truck driving job with crooked transport managers Cartley (William Hartnell) and Red (Patrick McGoohan). Yately finds the trucks in poor shape, the roads worse, and a quota system which requires him to drive at breakneck speeds to make a decent wage. He pals up with another driver, Gino (Herbert Lom) to get a better deal from the bosses, a liaison weakened by their common amour for the manager's secretary, Lucy (Peggy Cummins). Sidney James, Jill Ireland, Gordon Jackson, Sean Connery and David McCallum are included in the yarn which in execution borrows a fair bit from WAGES OF FEAR (viz. trucks suspended precariously over cliff edges, inter-driver rivalry, exploding trucks etc.)

Along with this array of good British acting stock, some of the UK industry's top technical crew put HELL DRIVERS together, including cameraman Geoffrey Unsworth and editor Ernest Archer. This ensured a quality product with those typically British touches that are hard to define but instantly recognisable.

Great Britain	1957	108 mins
Dir: C. Raker Endfield	*Prod:* John Kruse and Endfield	
Prod. Co: Rank/Aqua	*Script:* n/a	
Cast incl: Stanley Baker, Herbert Lom, Peggy Cummins, Patrick McGoohan, Wilfred Lawson, William Hartnell, Jill Ireland and Gordon Jackson		

HELL'S ANGELS ON WHEELS

Curious cycle gang exploiter with the as-yet undiscovered Jack Nicholson mugging his way through a heavy vernacular, HELL'S ANGELS ON WHEELS offered audiences little more than a seven course menu of Hell's Angels' initiation rites. No chickens' heads are bitten off, nor are there any graphic examples of perverse personal hygiene, but there *is* a lot of riding around in the desert and half-hearted fighting, all of it shot with a photographic sensitivity the script and ultra-nonchalant acting hardly warrant. Maybe director Richard Rush's employment of cameraman Laszlo Kovaks was his way of compensating for these glaring deficiencies, but it wasn't enough to save his film from the bottom division of the biker pic league.

USA	1967	95 mins
Dir: Richard Rush	*Prod:* Joe Solomon	
Prod. Co: U.S. Films	*Script:* Wright Campbell	
Cast incl: Jack Nicholson, Adam Roarke, Sabrina Scharf and John Garwood		

HELL'S ANGELS '69

Biker pic stalwarts Tom Stern and Jeremy Slate produced and wrote, as well as acted in HELL'S ANGELS '69 and as you might expect from these Peter Pans of the outlaw trade, the results were, well, different.

For a start, the Slate/Stern storyline is relatively imaginative, featuring our two rugged-browed heroes as a pair of spoilt brothers who decide to pose as Angels whilst executing a Las Vegas casino robbery. Although they ingratiate themselves adequately with the real biker gang, and the raid goes smoothly, the scapegoats don't realise that they're going to take the fall until Slate and Stern are laughing their way across the Nevada desert. If this is a sorry comment on the I.Q. of your average motorcycle buccaneer, it's one given added irony by Stern's casting, for he chose Sonny Barger, Terry The Tramp, Skip, Tiny, Magoo etc., etc., otherwise known as the infamous Oakland Hell's Angels, to play themselves! Of course when the penny *does* finally drop, they're after the brothers like a shot... and with murder in mind. Their venom is further thickened by the desertion of Angel mama, Betsy (Connie Van Dyke), who decided life might be better with a couple of smart rich boys than with a bunch of lumbering neanderthals. However the unlikely twist to HELL'S ANGELS '69 is that rather than beat Van Dyke and Slate to a pulp when they catch up with them, they merely take their gas and water and leave them to rot in the sand. This sophisticated sadism is something Stern fortunately avoids by the simple expedient of crashing his sickle in a righteously terminal manner.

Given that Barger, the Tramp and Co. can't really act, the three principals come on like members of the Royal Shakespeare Company by comparison. This, together with Lee Madden's efficient direction and a script which only falters seriously when the details of the actual raid are over-simplified, conspires to provide a memorable movie... if for all the wrong reasons.

USA   1969   96 mins
Dir: Lee Madden   *Prod:* Tom Stern
Prod. Co: Tracom   *Script:* Tom Stern, Jeremy Slate and Don Tait
Cast incl: Tom Stern, Jeremy Slate, Conny Van Dyke, J.D. Spradlin, Terry the Tramp, Sonny Barger, Skip, Tiny, Magoo and members of the Original Oakland Hell's Angels

Roarke and Slate again, this time with Slate as the good guy who's had his brand new Rickman Metisse (that's a rare but thoroughly unreliable British hybrid), stolen by Roarke via an intermediary (Michael Walker). Being a decent sort of a thieving outlaw biker, Roarke dumps his girlfriend (Jocelyn Lane) onto Slate by way of compensation. But despite this callous gesture, Ms. Lane displays a commendable loyalty to her ex-partner and will have little to do with the murderous pranks Slate directs at Roarke during the chase to retrieve his bike: snake-pit traps, rope trips, cascading boulders – nothing is beyond Slate's adolescent thirst for revenge. He even revives medieval jousting, with the two chaps battling it out with spiked chains on a strip of straight road.

We are also addressed with the unlikely hypothesis that Slate's manic desire to get his bike back is based on his desire to sell it and buy a ranch with the proceeds. I mean, what's he going to get for $2000 – a dog kennel in the middle of the Arizona desert? This is almost as implausible as the appearance of Ms. Lane and Angelique Prettyjohn (the latter having taken over from the former as Roarke's sleeping bag partner), whose clothing and make-up remains immaculate throughout all the nastiness. This is not entirely unconnected with the fact that American International later re-packaged the film as GIRL IN A MINI-SKIRT.

USA	1969	95 mins
Dir: Maury Dexter		*Prod:* Dexter
Prod. Co: American International		*Script:* James Gordon White and
		R.G. McMullen

Cast incl: Jeremy Slate, Adam Roarke, Jocelyn Lane, Angelique Prettyjohn, Michael Walker and Astrid Warner

IN COLOUR

Described by 'Variety' as "a well-knit programmer with juve interest", HOT ROD GIRL is in fact an horrendously moral placebo of a film which America's teenage brats would have doubtless assumed revealed all behind the glamorous facade and the padded bras of the drag racing crowd. What they got instead was Chuck Connors playing a cop who organises "official" speed trials to steer "the kids" away from anti-social, not to mention illegal, behaviour on the streets of California. Lori Nelson barely justifies the title role as the girlfriend of Jeff (John Smith – surely not his real name?), whose young brother is killed in one of those naughty street races. Connors is so cloyingly virtuous in his social worker role, that anyone seeing this film at the time of its release must have felt like going straight and having a chicken run down the main street. Daft.

> USA   1956   79 mins
> *Dir:* Leslie Martinson   *Prod:* Norman Herman
> *Prod. Co:* Nacirema Inc.   *Script:* John McGreevey
> *Cast incl:* Lori Nelson, John Smith, Chuck Connors, Frank Gorshin, Roxanne Arlen, Mark Andrews and Carol Kearney

HOT ROD RUMBLE

Leslie Martinson's quickie follow up to HOT ROD GIRL was originally put out on a double bill with something called CALYPSO JOE. HOT ROD RUMBLE was then described by one reviewer as "madcap youth stuff". Having to admit that I haven't actually seen it myself, I shall leave any critical assessment at that, but perhaps you should seek out this simple tale of street racing, mistaken identity and death on the highway if only for the performance of one, Richard Hartunian. This same reviewer claimed that Hartunian bore a strong resemblance in acting style and vocal delivery to Marlon Brando. I must admit I find it sad that this extraordinarily promising youngster disappeared without trace after his tumultous debut in HOT ROD RUMBLE! But then THE WILD ONE this is probably not.

> USA   1967   79 mins
> *Dir:* Leslie Martinson   *Prod:* Norman Herman
> *Prod. Co:* Nacirema Inc.   *Script:* Meyer Dolinsky
> *Cast incl:* Richard Hartunian, Leigh Snowden, Joey Forman, Brett Halsey and Larry Dolgin

HOT CARS

Twee little meller about a salesman who starts flogging stolen cars to pay medical bills for his ailing infant. Altogether now, say "Aaahh". Or perhaps that should be "Urgh!" Rubbish, whichever way you look at it.

USA   1956   60 mins
Dir: Donald McDougall   *Prod:* Howard W. Koch
Prod. Co: United Artists   *Script:* Don Martin and Richard Landau
Cast incl: John Bromfield, Joi Lansing, Mark Dana, Carol Shannon, Ralph Clanton and Dabbs Greer

HONKY TONK FREEWAY

A white elephant on wheels if ever there was one. Costing over $20M and precipitating the collapse of Lord Grade's American promotional arm, already bled dry by flops like RAISE THE TITANIC and CAN'T STOP THE MUSIC; HONKY TONK FREEWAY was a grotesque, big bucks parody of the exploitation movie. This John Schlesinger directed film spent its money not on big stars, but on grandiose special effects and stunts, requiring a huge crew and weeks of unanticipated production time. The story is about a small Florida town cut off by the nearby freeway and desperate to revive its tourist trade. The inhabitants resort to absurd gimmicks like painting the town pink, elephants on water skis and finally, dynamiting the freeway. This attracts a tourist boom never remotely planned for and the resultant traffic jam is a device Schlesinger and scripter Edward Clinton turn into what could be described as what would've happened if Walt Disney had made WEEKEND. A Bordello on wheels, promiscuous widows, drug abusing hitch-hikers, a man with a rhino in his boot, etc., etc. Funny it's not, mainly because the spectacle of all this whackiness is so blatantly and cynically contrived, that even an audience weaned on the weak slapstick and washroom humour of daytime television can see through it.

HONKY TONK FREEWAY must've been an embarrassment to all concerned: I even have trouble plucking up the nerve to admit I've seen it.

USA   1981   101 mins
Dir: John Schlesinger   *Prod:* Don Boyd
Prod. Co: Boyd Co   *Script:* Edward Clinton
Cast incl: Beau Bridges, Hume Cronyn, Geraldine Page, Teri Garr, William Devane, Joe Grifasi, Jessica Tandy and Paul Jabara

INDIANAPOLIS SPEEDWAY (a/k/a Roaring Road)

In this remake of Howard Hawks' THE CROWD ROARS, Ann Sheridan plays the Joan Blondell role and Pat O'Brien does a half-hearted impression of James Cagney as the kill-joy motor racer. Director Lloyd Bacon is no Howard Hawks either, and he adds nothing new to Hawks' original story. Even his direction of the racing scenes takes little account of the technical progress made during the seven years that elapsed between the two films. Remakes rarely work, and this one is certainly no exception.

USA   1939   82 mins
Dir: Lloyd Bacon   *Prod. Co:* Warner Bros.
Script: Sig Heraig and Wally Klein
Cast incl: Pat O'Brien, Ann Sheridan, John Payne, Cale Page, Frank McHugh, Grace Staffor and Granville Bates

JACKSON COUNTY JAIL

New World productions are not known to be intellectually provocative – provocative, perhaps, but intellectual, *no*! However JACKSON COUNTY JAIL is a rarity inasmuch as it utilises familiar Corman shock tactics, but applies them to a storyline that challenges certain commonly held values.

Yvette Mimieux stars as an affluent executive in a Beverly Hills advertising agency. She's got a good career producing the sort of ads that depict women like her as role models, and a lover who cheats on her. Being a smart sort of girl, she decides to leave this empty lifestyle behind her and move to the east coast. And she decides to drive. However this is a decision she takes not because she's anxious to find that ambiguous "something" that is the staple of numerous road movies, but rather that she's a bit of a voyeur... looking for trouble, in fact. And trouble she gets in spades.

Firstly, she picks up two seedy hippies (Robert Carradine and Frederick Cook), who beat her up, steal her car and leave her in an amoral red-neck town where she's jailed on vagrancy charges, and then raped by the psychotic jailer. Having killed him in self-defence, she escapes with fellow-internee, Coley Blake (Tommy Lee Jones, in much the same role he played in BACK ROADS), whose justification for his criminal activities is that "everyone is dishonest". After much chasing around by a bunch of hoodlum cops, Blake is killed when the two fugitives are cornered in the midst of a bi-centennial parade. The film closes with Mimieux looking aghast at his lifeless body as she waits to be driven off in a police-car, presumably to an unspeakable future.

The rape scene which is central to JACKSON COUNTY JAIL is handled with restraint and with a strong committment to the woman's point of view – which is, of course, one of sheer terror and disgust. For a Corman film, this is quite remarkable and first-time director Mike Miller and Yvette Mimieux must be congratulated for resisting the prurience of films like LIPSTICK and STRAW DOGS. Throughout the film, Mimieux carries herself with a nicely fragile confidence, trying to maintain the poise that drew approbation in Los Angeles, but targets her for ridicule and chastisement in a resentful, immoral little backwater like Jackson County. She perfectly conveys the helpless fear of watching her nice, nouveau-riche world crumble around her and, whilst much of Donald Stewart's script implies that maybe this is no bad thing, once she's in jail and faced by the prospect of rape, Mimieux loses her false West Coast certitude and responds like any other intelligent woman would. Or does she? The right to kill her rapist was questioned by many when the film first appeared and sparked off a fiery debate between feminists and legal experts, the latter arguing that since the Mimieux character was out for a taste of low-life in the first place, she was in part responsible for what happened.

This is one of the ambiguities that pepper Jackson County Jail, adding dimensions to the story, and indeed the production and performances, which notably stretch the genre.

USA   1976   89 mins
Dir: Michael Miller   *Prod:* Jeff Begun and Roger Corman
Prod. Co: New World   *Script:* Donald Stewart
Cast incl: Yvette Mimieux, Tommy Lee Jones, Robert Carradine, Frederic Cook, Severn Darden, John Lawlor, Howard Hesseman, Mary Woronov and Britt Leach

DINAH HUNTER (YVETTE MIMIEUX) changes clothes in a Caravan hideaway whilst on the run from the police in "JACKSON COUNTY JAIL" a United Artists release.

JOYRIDE

I imagine there must have been a few spats during the making of JOYRIDE, the film's four protagonists all being off-spring of famous names – the only one you may not immediately recognise is Melanie Griffith, daughter of Tippi Hedren. Together with Desi Arnez Jr., Robert Carradine and Ann Lockhart, Ms. Griffith stars in a bleak little meller about kids who decide to leave their hum-drum homelife in Los Angeles and drive up to Alaska. Freedom, in their case, is a dirty, inhospitable pipeline town, but their adventures during and after the trip there are anything but uplifting. The usual round of casual sex (sometimes on the car hood!) and teenage pranks degenerates into prostitution, robbery with violence and Lockhart being held as a (willing) hostage.

Okay, it's a little more dramatic than the hot-rod/beach party films to which it is a natural heir, but JOYRIDE is still a pretty facile concept. Responsibility for this must rest fairly and squarely with Joseph Ruben, who scripted and directed the pic (he was also involved with the dire POM-POM GIRLS), for the kids from Beverly Hills do their best to keep their roles in the realms of realism.

USA   1977   92 mins
Dir: Joseph Ruben   *Prod:* Bruce Cohn Curtis
Prod. Co: Landers-Roberts   *Script:* Peter Rainer and Ruben
Cast incl: Desi Arnez Jr., Anne Lockhart, Melanie Griffith, Robert Carradine, Tom Ligon and Cliff Lenz

KINGS OF THE ROAD

A road movie by one of the young masters of the German cinema, Wim Wenders, adds nothing to the genre except a mantle of despair, cast with none of Strick's contrivance (ROAD MOVIE) nor Malick's subtlety (BADLANDS).

The excruciatingly long (176 minutes) KINGS OF THE ROAD chronicles the progress of a projector mechanic who travels to a succession of small town cinemas across the plains of West Germany. Bruno (Ruediger Vogler) is unable to communicate anything to the world, except through his work. This is best illustrated by a short interlude of empty romance with a cinema cashier (Lisa Kreuzer), which confirms his sexual as well as his emotional impotence. Robert, the hitchhiker he picks up and eventually makes his assistant (played by Hanns Zischler), demonstrates *his* own estrangement from reality during a meeting with his father (Rudolf Schuendler); instead of voicing his enmity towards him, he makes up a page of type from his father's newspaper plant and leaves the printed word for him to read in the morning. Eventually the two travellers part company: Robert dejectedly returns to the life he found so aimless after his wife left him. Bruno continues on his way in his large, awkward van. Wenders' script offers no conclusions from their experiences together, and not enough clues for the audience to draw its own.

KINGS is an existential conundrum, adrift and humourless in a wanly photographed landscape, through which it crawls at a snail's pace. Perhaps the film is best summed up by one of Wenders' little visual jokes, at least I assume it's a joke: a man defecating in a quartz mine, the dark faeces dropping ponderously, symbolically, onto the white stone.

Germany	1976	176 mins
Dir: Wim Wenders		*Prod:* Wenders
Script: Wenders		

Cast incl: Ruediger Vogler, Hanns Zischler, Lisa Kruezer, Rudolf Schuendler and Marquard Bohm

THE LAST AMERICAN HERO

THE LAST AMERICAN HERO presents us with an America where motor racing is accepted as an integral, if not actually essential, part of life. This is not the glitzy world of leggy models and aerodynamic drag factors seen in films like GRAND PRIX and LE MANS, but the tough, grizzled face of a truly American phenomenon – stockcar racing. Director Lamont Johnson paid careful attention to the parochial appeal of the big, saloon-based cars and the men who barrel them round the banked ovals at speeds up to 200 mph. His racing footage is closely observed and exudes the appropriate visceral qualities, yet it never even starts to overwhelm the storyline. And the plot is an equally well perceived, often touching, examination of innocence lost somewhere between the backwoods of North Carolina, and Detroit's star-hungry motorsports industry.

Jeff Bridges plays Junior Jackson, a role based loosely on Junior Johnson, the hugely successful NASCAR champion and subject of an 'Esquire' article by Tom Wolfe which inspired the script. Jackson delivers moonshine whisky for his father (Art Lund), and the film opens with an epic woodlands chase between Jackson and some obviously outclassed Treasury agents. The law, sick of being humiliated by the fast-running Jackson family, destroys the old man's still and throws him in jail. Motivated by a mixture of guilt and pride, Junior decides to put his driving skills to good use and enters a demolition derby. To improve his chances, he builds a hydraulic battering ram into his car, which leads to a win alright, and also a disqualification. This galvanises his resolve and, together with his brother Wayne (Gary Busey, acquitting himself far better than he did in ANGELS DIE HARD), he builds a stockcar and finances his efforts by operating a moonshine delivery business. Determined to retain the independence instilled in him by his dad, Junior eschews an offer of sponsorship, and as a surprise for his father when he leaves jail, he and Wayne build an underground still for him. But Jackson Snr. doesn't want any of them to continue living with the threat of prison hanging over his head, and symbolically destroys the still. After an unsatisfactory affair with a racing groupie (Valerie Perrine) for whom he fell too hard, Junior is left despondent and car-less. Eventually he decides to accept sponsorship after all, but for a percentage of the take. He wins his first race, demands and gets a higher cut for further outings, and is asked at the press conference which ends the film, "Where you goin' from here, Junior?"

The affinity between father and son is a theme rarely developed in an era of movie-making primarily concerned with emotional alienation and wilful independence, but here it's a relationship that's mutually supportive and respectful, rather than protective and soppy. "Damn foolishness to one man is breath of life to another," says Jackson Snr., complimenting his son's desire to risk his all motor racing, rather than settle down as a garage mechanic. His fears are not so much for his son's health on the race track, but for his ability to stay out of jail. But even he admits that he'll carry on moonshining, because he "don't know nothing else."

Junior's ascension to pro-racing is accompanied by a failure to take his buddies with him, and his tacit admission of their relative immaturity is a beautifully, even poignantly executed scene. So is the biggest set-back in his otherwise upward mobility, his spurning by Marge, the stockcar slut. "You're still my darlin' " she tells him when she exits their motel room, and Junior does some fast growing up as he grapples with such capricious sexual allegiance.

Jeff Bridges' folksy ebullience is even better suited to Junior Jackson than it was to the cocksure drifter in THUNDERBOLT & LIGHTFOOT. Indeed all the actors are perfectly suited to the simple, but hardly innocent, lifestyle their characters subscribe to, with Ed Lauter ascribing just the right degree of contrast as the cunning regional sponsor, Burton Colt. A finely crafted, unassuming but nonetheless confident movie, THE LAST AMERICAN HERO may well betray a grain of truth in its title: as Detroit re-tools for the internationally uniform econo-cars of the future, stockcar racing and its gosh-darn ambience are doomed to fade away. This film remains as a useful epitaph.

USA   1973   95 mins
Dir: Lamont Johnson   *Prod:* William Roberts
Prod. Co: Wizan/Rojo   *Script:* Roberts
Photog: George Silano   *Stunt Dir:* Everett Creach
Cast incl: Junior Jackson – Jeff Bridges; Elroy Jackson – Art Lund; Mrs. Jackson – Geraldine Fitzgerald; Wayne Jackson – Gary Busey; Marge – Valerie Perrine; Burton Colt – Ed Lauter; Hackel – Ned Beatty; also featuring Gregory Walcott, Tom Ligon, Ernie Orsatti, Erica Hagen and James Murphy

THE LAST RIDE

In the aftermath of World War I, a gang of crooks profit from the rubber shortage by selling high-priced, low-quality re-tread tyres. But Richard Travis, as a diligent lieutenant detective, gets on their case after one of the tyres bursts, killing a couple of children. And the tyres are not the only commodity that is paper-thin in THE LAST RIDE; plot, screenplay and acting are all woefully inadequate. And as the film was conceived as a support feature, director D. Ross Lederman pumps as much tyre-squealing, gun-firing action as he can into his 54 minutes, which leaves the exposition of the story and the characterisations at their most rudimentary.
Dismal.

USA   1944   54 mins
Dir: D. Ross Lederman   *Prod. Co:* Warner Bros.
Script: Lederman
Cast incl: Richard Travis, Charles Lang, Eleanor Parker, Jack La Rue, Cy
        Kendall and Wade Boteler

THE LAST RUN

The ending of Richard Fleischer's THE LAST RUN transposes the identities of a man and his car in a thoroughly obtuse manner; with the demise of one, the other is rendered lifeless. This bit of theatrical overstatement spoils what has hitherto been a well essayed relationship between George C. Scott and his BMW 503. In THE LAST RUN the car is as essential to the mood and the exposition of the film which is, as might be suspected, about the perfidy of forced alliances.

Scott, as an ageing underworld getaway driver, agrees to help a convict escape from a Spanish jail and deliver him to a rendezvous in France. Tony Musante, playing the escapee, persuades Scott to pick up his girlfriend (Trish Van Devere)

along the way, and the movie chronicles their deepening and perverse dependency on each other. (Which includes a bondage scene the censors must have completely misinterpreted back in the innocent days of 1971).

The keynote of THE LAST RUN is, at least until the over-blown demise of Scott and his faithful vehicle, a subtlety that extends through script, acting and photography. Even the stunt driving largely avoids sensationalising what are, in fact, the exhilarating consequences of fast, expert driving. And George C. Scott was apparently so taken with the BMW during filming that he went out and bought one afterwards.

USA   1971   92 mins
Dir: Richard Fleischer   *Prod:* Carter de Haven
Prod. Co: MGM/De Haven   *Script:* Alan Sharp
Cast incl: George C. Scott, Tony Musante, Trish Van Devere, Colleen
Dewhurst, Aldo Sanbrell and Antonio Tarruella

THE LEATHER BOYS

Considering the cinema nowadays regards homosexuality as an acceptable alternative to hetrosexuality, it's hard to believe that mild references to latent faggotry caused a year's delay between completion and distribution of THE LEATHER BOYS. Yet that's how long it took censors and studio officials to agonise over its release, such were the taboos of the early 'sixties. However, director Sidney Furie carefully avoided making the subject controversial, treating the relationship between two young adolescents as dispassionately as he observed life in working-class Britain in which they were growing up. Without approval or condemnation, Furie's direction and Gillian Freeman's incisive script let the young cast make the most of their situation and the audience its own social and moral judgements.

Reggie (Colin Campbell) marries Dot (Rita Tushingham) straight after leaving school, and after a holiday camp honeymoon during which Dot's sluttish tendencies give Reggie his first doubts about connubial bliss, he moves back to live with his grandmother. It's there he meets Pete (Dudley Sutton), a fellow biker who he's obliged to share a room with. Encouraged by their common interest in bikes, their relationship flourishes and Reggie has all but forgotten Dot until he runs into her again when they all find themselves taking part in a frantic motorcycle race to Edinburgh. Despite reservations, Dot and Reggie decide to get back together again, but when they enter her flat to find another boy in her bed, Reggie runs back to Pete for sympathy and support. The two of them make plans to sail off for a new life in America, but an incident with one of Pete's old "friends" at Southampton Docks clears up any doubts Reggie had about his sexual intentions. Repelled by this, and confused about his own emotional and sexual identity, Reggie finds himself truly alone for the first time in his life, and well on the way to becoming an adult.

Unlike Furie's later motorcycle drama, LITTLE FAUSS AND BIG HALSY, THE LEATHER BOYS is well organised and credible – even the actual riding sequences reek of burning oil and ton-up bravura. As a reflection of a society groping towards affluence and self-assurance, it's also a pretty astute effort that rarely patronises or occludes the very Britishness of its characters. Much credit must go to the actors for this, especially Rita Tushingham as the bug-eyed, back-street coquette who manages to convey both the despair of premature marriage and a cheeky optimism. She's the strongest character in the film, the only one who has really got a grasp of their identity, although she realises it too late to save Reggie from himself. The insidious implications of the bond between Reggie and Pete may have made a few motorcyclists uncomfortable, but by and large the gay symbolism is kept to a minimum. The same cannot be said, I'm afraid, of the back projection.

Britain   1963   108 mins
Dir: Sidney J. Furie   *Prod:* Raymond Stross
Prod. Co: Garrick/British Lion   *Script:* Gillian Freeman
Cast incl: Rita Tushingham, Colin Campbell, Dudley Sutton, Gladys
          Henson, Lockwood West, Betty Marsden, Avice Landon,
          Martin Matthews and Dandy Nichols

LE MANS

Having fêted LE MANS as an exemplar of motor racing movies in my introduction, I won't bother to repeat myself here. What I omitted to mention from my earlier reference, however, was an outline of the plot, scant though it is.

Michael Delaney (Steve McQueen) is first seen apprehensively viewing the scene of an accident he survived twelve months earlier at the Le Mans 24 Hours race. Shortly thereafter, he returns to the track as the star member of the Gulf/Porsche team, and is in the forefront of this year's race when a moment's slipped concentration renders him victim of yet another accident. He hurts his knee slightly, but totals his car. Despondent in his caravan, he tries to explain to the widow of an ex-racing colleague (Elga Andersen) what it is that compels men like him to take up such a dangerous sport. Before he has a chance to finish, he's called out to replace a fatigued team-mate and, of course, goes on to win.

LE MANS is the quintessential movie for the motor racing fan: it chronicles the world's most famous endurance race, much of it run on public roads sealed off for the occasion, and graphically highlights the pressures and meticulous support systems – human and otherwise – inherent in such a spectacle. But the emotional side of things is also given its place, not just in the exchange between Andersen and McQueen, but also in the nervy dependency between team-mates, mechanics and managers. The photography is nothing short of sensational, and director Lee Katzin cleverly combined the natural sounds of the racing, the sideshows and even McQueen's heartbeats merging them evocatively with Michel Legrand's soundtrack music.

USA   1971   100 mins
Dir: Lee Katzin   *Prod:* Jack L. Reddish
Prod. Co: Solar   *Script:* Harry Kleiner
Cast incl: Steve McQueen, Elga Andersen, Siegfried Rauch, Ronald
          Leigh-Hunt, Fred Haltiner, Luc Merenda, Christopher Waite,
          Louise Edlind and Jean-Claude Bercq

LITTLE FAUSS AND BIG HALSY

The title characters of this movie are a disingenuous braggart of a motorcycle racer, Halsy Knox (Robert Redford), and the shy, would-be racer he tricks into becoming his mechanic, Little Fauss (Michael J. Pollard). With Fauss in his thrall, Halsy takes off on the motorcycling equivalent of JUNIOR BONNER's rodeo circuit, scratching a living from prize money and other riders' misfortunes. They are soon joined by Rita Nebraska (Lauren Hutton), a rich bohemian attracted by Halsy's swaggering manner and, it seems, the lengthy scar down his back. Edged out of the relationship by Rita's arrival, Fauss realises how much he's been exploited and eventually returns home to stake out his own racing career. Ever on the look out for a fall-guy, Halsy can't resist the temptation to seek out Fauss and try and dump the now pregnant Rita on him, but Fauss pluckily rebuffs him. He further establishes his maturity and independence by winning a big race, after Halsy's poorly maintained bike breaks down.

Redford, as the all-round Mr. Nasty, and Michael J. Pollard, virtually re-creating the willingly put-upon character he played in BONNIE AND CLYDE, give professional and even excellent performances, especially when Fauss is dealing with his parents (Noah Beery and Lucille Benson in charming little cameos). But Lauren Hutton overplays the spoilt brat to the point that the chemistry between the three of them slides into parody. Why would she be attracted to Halsy if not just for a quick lay? Why would she entertain someone like Fauss as a surrogate father? Charles Eastman asks neither of these questions in his script, and the weak dynamics of the characterisation provide no clue to the possible answers.

The atmosphere of semi-pro motorcycle racing is fairly well conveyed by Sidney Furie, but the racing footage resorts all too willingly to back projection and a few expensive camera tricks. However, there is one line in the script which motorcyclists the world over will probably identify with, when Little Fauss expounds his aim in life: "I just want to race motorcycles and screw people."

Right on!

USA   1970   99 mins.
Dir: Sidney J. Furie   *Prod:* Albert Ruddy
Prod. Co: Alfran/Furie Prods.   *Script:* Charles Eastman
Cast incl: Robert Redford, Michael J. Pollard, Noah Beery, Lucille Benson, Lauren Hutton, Ray Ballard and Erin O'Reilly

THE LIVELY SET

As far as I'm aware, THE LIVELY SET is the only movie ever to feature jet-powered dragsters as a dramatic pivot. It's also the only one to feature Joanie Somers singing custom-written tunes by Bobby Darin, and the only one to feature a world land-speed record holder in an "acting role", and that's Mickey Thomas.

That apart, THE LIVELY SET is one of those girl-takes-a-backseat-to-car racing movies, with the requisite amount of male rivalry, and rather more than enough gee-whizz technology. Some-time pop singer James Darren scolding his university physics professor for knowing nothing, but *nothing* about gas turbine engines stretches the storyline's credibility to the limit. Newsreel footage of Bonneville record attempts and half-assed acting (with the possible exception of the slab-jawed Dough McClure), plunges the film into ennui, but then how much dynamism and excitement should we really expect from something called THE LIVELY SET, for heavens sake?

USA   1964   90 mins.
Dir: Jack Arnold   *Prod:* William Alland
Prod. Co: Universal   *Script:* Mel Goldberg and William Wood
Cast incl: James Darren, Pamela Tiffin, Doug McClure, Joanie Summers, Marilyn Maxwell, Charles Drake and Russ Conway

THE LONG HAUL

The abiding image of THE LONG HAUL is one of 'fifties glamour puss Diana Dors wearing a mink coat, sitting in the cab of a dirty Leyland truck being driven by the portly Victor Mature. The idea of these two non-actors steamrollering through an implausible script, with Ms. Dors as a cafe proprietor and gangster's moll and Mr. Mature as an unwilling fur smuggler, makes for an irresistible piece of kitsch.

THE LONG HAUL was directed by a young Ken Hughes from his own screenplay, which cast big Vic as an ex-serviceman stranded in Blighty with a wife (Gene Anderson) whose child is of "dubious parentage". He gets a job driving trucks for mobster Patrick Allen, but makes the mistake of falling for Allen's girl, that's Diana of course. The illicit fur run is designed to buy freedom for the two cheating lovers, but plans naturally go awry.

Still, our interest is maintained by the frequent ripping of Diana's wardrobe (hardly surprising since she's the sort of girl who wears sequinned ball gowns in transport caffs), and the sight of her wading waist deep through a Scottish river. Boy, does that girl suffer. Mature also pays for his transgressions by having his arm crushed by a truck, getting hit a lot by everyone, and eventually going to jail. Both stars respond to their ordeals with expressionless stares that should not be mistaken for stoicism; they just daren't move a muscle in case something cracks or twangs.

THE LONG HAUL – a fine advertisement for British corsetry and pancake make-up.

Britain   1957   100 mins.
Dir: Ken Hughes   *Prod:* Maxwell Setton
Prod. Co: Setton/Columbia   *Script:* Hughes
Cast incl: Victor Mature, Diana Dors, Patrick Allen, Gene Anderson,
          Peter Reynolds, Liam Redmond, John Welsh, Murray Kash,
          Meior Tzelniker and Michael Wade

THE LOSERS

Jack Starrett goes straight in this one, eshewing his carefully dirtied Angel "originals" for the white suit of an American CIA agent, and also the director's chair. Yet this *is* a biker movie, but the outlaws themselves have undergone a half-cocked metamorphosis, winding up as Yankee guerrillas sent to liberate Starrett from behind enemy lines in Vietnam. The ridiculous premise of Alan Caillou's script, namely that only a motley cycle gang are butch enough to accomplish such a rescue, doesn't help the credibility of erstwhile Harley-Davidson riders sent buggering about the jungle on pip-squeak Yamaha trail bikes... even if they are fitted with machine guns! They look, well, stupid. And they look even more stupid when they've gone through hell, highwater and the sort of wistful circumspection that's only possible on the Orient, only to find that Starrett doesn't want to leave... "He's happy here etc., etc."

Occasionally funny for its sheer absurdity, THE LOSERS starts to lose water after you've seen a trailbike jump through the air for the fifth time and watched Adam Roarke going dewey-eyed over a demure native girl. And it's not even well made, although a team of (patently) veteran biker pic actors do their struggling best.

USA   1970   95 mins.
Dir: Jack Starrett   *Prod:* Joe Solomon
Prod. Co: Fanfare Prods.   *Script:* Alan Caillou
Cast incl: William Smith, Bernie Hamilton, Adam Roarke, Houston
          Savage, Jack Starrett, Paul Koslo and Gene Cornelius

MAD MAX & MAD MAX II

Sequels are notoriously hard to pull-off, but Byron Kennedy's production of MAD MAX II far surpasses the original.

Much as Sergio Leone created a timeless hero in Clint Eastwood's MAN WITH NO NAME, Director George Miller and his co-scriptwriter, Terry Hayes, came up with a great concept, the avenging angel of the post-oil age. Topical at a time of middle eastern armed conflict, MAD MAX was set in a world laid to industrial and economic ruin by the ultimate in oil wars. Gangs of mechanized marauders roam across the wasted landscapes, killing for a few precious gallons of petrol, challanged only by a few brave lawmen. Max, played by Mel Gibson, is a former highway patrolman whose commitment to combat these packs of wild outlaws is hardened by the death of his wife and child at the hands of one such gang. Max's random vendetta forms the bulk of this first film, a bloody odyssey involving helmeted, armour-suited psychopaths that extend the Hell's Angel mythology into a culture of sadism, steel and the great god gasoline.

MAD MAX II opens with a flashback synopsis of its predecessor and is set some three years later, the police force having totally collapsed and Max, a lone, Robin Hood-type figure, still driving the patched-up remnants of the super-charged pursuit car he had as a cop. An initial skirmish with a bike gang, led by the Mohican-coiffered Wez (Vernon Wells), gets Max some much-needed juice and leads to a confrontation with an eccentric gyro-copter pilot (Bruce Spence – who also featured in THE CARS THAT ATE PARIS). In return for sparing his life, Gyro takes Max to a rocky outcrop where they can see a bizarre battle taking place in the desert beyond. Dozens of outlaws aboard a variety of bizarre bikes and armoured vehicles are attacking a barbed wire fortress in which a group of latter-day hippie capitalists are defending a small oil-refinery. One of their number leaves the compound as a decoy to divert the assailants, most of whom are armed with powerful crossbows. He is attacked and left for dead, but Max saves him and manages to get him back to the refinery, using him as a passport. Max tells the refinery people that he knows of an abandoned oil tanker which he will bring to them, if they give him all the fuel he can carry. This coincides with a threat from the marauder's leader, the sinister Humungus (Kjell Nilsson), that if they leave and give up their refinery, he'll guarantee them a safe passage through the lands he controls. They have 24 hours to consider, otherwise he'll

invade. That night Max escapes through a tunnel carrying jerry cans full of fuel for the tanker. Aided by Gyro, he makes it back to the refinery and after further warring with the outlaws, Max is asked to help the refinery people make their highly dangerous flight. He refuses and takes off in his own car with the promised fuel. After being attacked and badly injured by the Humungus, his car is blown up and he regains consciousness back in the compound, having been found and ferried there by Gyro. Subsequently he demands to drive the tanker in its escape. The climactic road and desert battle is quintessential mobile carnage – not for the squeamish – with a horribly ironic denouement.

MAD MAX II benefits considerably from the production team's experience on the first film: the action sequences are more effective and often stunning, the storyline better resolved and, with more money available, the rituals and artefacts of this grim, lawless new society are graphically explicated The outlaw vehicles are well constructed with a sci-fi illustrator's sense of the bizarre (although there's more than a touch of the Kawasaki 900s to many of the bikes). The outlaws themselves suggest a cross-fertilisation 'twixt punk, Hell's Angel and medieval knight. Mel Gibson as Max really does fall into the Eastwood mould of the sardonic, slightly sadistic avenger, but underplays his role just enough to humanize it, rather like Harrison Ford in RAIDERS OF THE LOST ARK. The direction, too, exhibits a kind of dark hubris, and never gets bogged down in the gratuitous gore that spoilt the original MAD MAX.

Together with ROAD GAMES, the two MAX's are fine evidence of Australia's burgeoning road movie industry!

Australia   1981   95 mins.
Dir: George Miller   *Prod:* Byron Kennedy
Prod. Co: Warner Bros *Script:* Terry Hayes, Brian Hannant and Miller
Cast incl: Mel Gibson, Bruce Spence, Vernon Wells, Emil Minty, Kjell
     Nilsson, Mike Preston, Virginia Hey, Syd Heylen and Moira
     Claux

OUTLAW BLUES

Scripted by B.W.L. Norton immediately before he wrote CONVOY, OUTLAW BLUES tackles several of the same topics (police corruption, elusive justice and romance on the run), but with considerably more sagacity. Whereas in CONVOY, the ideas were apparently plucked out of the air the morning of the shoot, the story of Bobby Ogden's quest for justice is intelligently conceived and presents its characters as individuals, rather than caricatures of a cartoonist's making.

Peter Fonda plays Ogden, an ex-convict out to get the country and western singer (James Callahan) who's profited hugely from a song he played to him at a prison concert. He finally apprehends the singer, but accidently wounds him in a brawl, making Ogden a wanted man again, and also the sort of underdog that seen-it-all backing singer Susan St. James is strangely moved by (especially in the region of her loins). Using her showbiz savvy, she helps him get his just desserts by organising an audacious series of live gigs where the couple are always just one jump ahead of the cops. The resultant publicity wins Ogden a huge sympathy vote and ultimately, justice is done. The moral of this being, I suppose, that if you're in showbiz, you get better treatment from the judiciary.

That little irony aside, OUTLAW BLUES is a successful and economic little thriller. Neither of the lead players are great actors, but they pass for real and the cheery insolence of Norton's script, Richard Heffron's direction and Cary Loftin's stunt work, carries them along nicely when they can't draw on innate theatricality alone.

(Fraud not to road movie afficiandos: arguably the best action sequence in OUTLAW BLUES is a boat chase!)

USA	1977	102 mins

Dir: Richard T. Heffron　　　　　　　　　　　　　　　*Prod:* Paul Heller
Prod. Co: Warner Bros.　　　　　　　　　　　　　　　*Script:* B.W.L. Norton
Cast incl: Peter Fonda, Susan St. James, John Crawford, James Callahan,
　　　　　Michael Lerner, Steve Fromholz, Richard Lockmiller and
　　　　　Matt Clark

PAPER MOON

Now here is an exploitation film of a rather different stripe from the gals, gore and gang warfare usually associated with B-feature road movies. And although it received almost unanimous critical praise when it was first released, PAPER MOON is a safe, predictable story, safely and predictably executed. Which is not to deny its qualities as a road movie, which are quite considerable, but someone has to point out that one man's road movie is another man's tear-jerker.

PAPER MOON's storyline engages our sympathies for the lovable con-man, in this case Ryan O'Neal, who sells bibles to the recently widowed by scanning the death notices in local newspapers. Driving through depression-wracked Kansas and Missouri in his pleasant ramshackle Model-T roadster, he comes up across a lisping cherub (his real-life daughter, Tatum), who is herself fairly adept at easing a few bucks out of gullible purses. She smokes, she curses, she has her own stated ethics... and she looks so goddamn Shirley Temple-*cute*. How I hate this child. Adding more sugar to her already syrupy role is the suggestion that this precocious nipper may be O'Neal's off-spring, abandoned in order to protect her from his sordid lifestyle. As might be expected from this pairing, their adventures together are a rising tide of moist-eyed bosh which nearly drowns the callous sceptic in a denouement of decency and morality.

None of this is very different from numerous other films which play on cosy assumptions we all make about good triumphing over evil, the girl getting the guy with the heart of steel, the beleaguered family who enjoy a sudden windfall. We're talking family market, we're talking big box office, and I dislike it because it challenges none of the safe premises of human nature and panders only to the lowest common denominator. In PAPER MOON, the confidence trickster is redeemed because he charges for his bibles only what he thinks his widows can afford – on one noble occasion actually delivering a copy free to a particularly wretched mum. His juvenile cohort is also ultimately harmless because she is a poor little *waif*, and, perhaps, his daughter.

The film is just about saved by its monochrome portrait of America in the 'thirties, and like Arthur Penn's BONNIE AND CLYDE, every saloon bar, every frontage and every frock is quietly but unerringly accurate. The driving and the in-car dialogue between our two foppish rogues link the bathos together as efficiently as they provide an excuse for the camera's poetic vistas: if you can stomach the rest of this two-hankie weepy, the driving and the decor are worth it.

USA 1973 94 mins
Dir: Peter Bogdanovich *Prod:* Alvin Sargent
Prod. Co: Saticoy/Paramount *Script:* Sargent
Cast incl: Ryan O'Neal, Tatum O'Neal, Madeleine Kahn and John Hillerman

PAY DAY

Maury Dann, the second-class country'n'western star is hardly PAY DAY's hero in the conventional sense, but in his sheer, unrelieved malignance, he exudes an oddly compelling charm. Darryl Duke's film follows him and his entourage for 18 hours travel through Alabama, and in that time we are privy to scenes of arrogance, sadistic guile, hypocrisy and a relentless abuse of almost anyone he comes into contact with. Brilliantly played by Rip Torn, Dann commands his seedy little empire from the rear of his Cadillac, slurping bourbon and popping speed, seducing a groupie while his "real" girlfriend sleeps next to him – and when she wakes up and protests, he throws her out of the car. People only mean something to Maury Dann if he can use them, thus the mutual loyalty between himself and his black chauffeur, Chicago (Cliff Emmich) is abruptly terminated when Dann gets him to take the rap for a restaurant knifing he got involved in. He feeds his already wasted mother with more pep pills, and his ex-wife with more reasons for hating him. He bribes and sweet-talks his way out of trouble and into the limelight, and Torn plays the part with a kind of mean, lascivious enthusiasm that would beg moral vilification were it not for two important considerations.

Firstly, Dann is the only thing of any substance in a tacky and unreformed world where people search constantly for The Main Chance at the expense of everything else. There are repeated suggestions that the restauranteur he pays off and the dee-jays he coerces would do exactly the same if they had Maury Dann's nerve. But they don't, and the ethics of these situations barely flicker through their minds. The other ambivalent aspect of Dann's behaviour is the knowledge that it just can't go on, that he *must* meet a sticky end, and Duke's clipped, urgent pace and Don Carpenter's highly efficient script (and for once I'm not using that phrase as veiled criticism), hurtle him on to his downfall with a gasping certainty.

I love this film for the accuracy of its insights, both into the fake sincerity of the music business, and the pattern of American road life (which has none of BACK ROADS' tinsel and little of ROAD MOVIE's resentment). And I can't help but admire the empathy the major actors seem to have for their characters: Ahna Capri as Dann's long suffering mistress; Cliff Emmich, who brings a pathetic dignity to the doomed chauffeur; and Michael Gwynne, as his subservient manager. Duke, a documentary and t.v. director whose first theatrical effort this was, helped producer/writer Don Carpenter bring in PAY DAY for well under 800,00 dollars. They did it by shooting entirely on location and using local amateurs for many of the minor roles, and very convincingly, too.

The film's executive producer was the late Ralph J. Gleason, a director of Fantasy Records at the time, and a highly respected jazz and rock columnist for many years before that. Gleason's contacts and his knowledge of the business ensured that everything about PAY DAY's scenarios and vernacular was steeped in reality, and without betraying its low budget.

The only comparison that springs readily to mind is THE PRIVATE FILES OF J. EDGAR HOOVER, for there is a direct parallel between the twisted authority of Broderick Crawford's Hoover and Rip Torn's Maury Dann. But beyond PAY DAY's powerful central figure, this harsh, disturbing film echoes the messages of EASY RIDER and VANISHING POINT in telling us something about the greater morality of a nation motivated by greed.

USA   1972   103 mins
Dir: Daryl Duke   *Prod:* Don Carpenter and Martin Fink
Prod. Co: Pumice Finance/Fantasy Films   *Script:* Carpenter
Cast incl: Rip Torn, Ahna Capri, Michael C. Gwynne, Jeff Morris, Cliff
                Emmich, Clara Dunn, Eleanor Fell, Henry O. Arnold, Linda
                Spatz and Walter Bamberg

RADIO ON

Generally respected, even revered, by British critics, I myself find Chris Petit's RADIO ON irritatingly derivative and almost without cinematic virtue.

The film's central charcter is Robert, who morosely works a night-shift as a dee-jay at a London biscuit factory. One morning he returns to the flat he shares with a quarrelsome girlfriend, played by Sue Jones Davies, to receive a phone-call from his mother, telling him his brother is dead. Robert lounges about looking moody (a pose he maintains throughout the film), but eventually drives off to Bristol in the South West of England where his brother died, presumably to check things out. Gratuitously arty aerial and panoramic shots of London accompany his departure in his old Rover 95, and it's not long before he picks up an army deserter in a roadside pub, which occasions some equally indulgent polemic about the brutality of the war in Belfast. After dumping the squaddy and exchanging some glib reminiscences about Eddie Cochran with the attendant in a country filling station (played by the Police's singer, Sting), Robert eventually arrives at his late brother's flat. There he finds another irascible female, who reveals little detail of his brother's demise in an exchange which fails to invoke the air of mystery it was doubtless supposed to. Robert goes out, buys a hot dog for a small brat who improbably recites a line from Cochran's 'Three Steps To Heaven', and fails to enter a rock club. Gripping stuff, eh? He then meets two German girls, Lisa Kreuzer and Katja Kersten, the former of whom is searching the West Country for the child her estranged husband has evidently abducted. They talk gloomily in the girls' hotel room. The next day, Robert visits Weston-Super-Mare with the Kreuzer woman, has tea with her husband's mother whilst the two women argue in German (no subtitles) and returns to Bristol. That night he is assaulted by a punkish female snooker player in a docklands bar. The next day he runs out of petrol on a cliff edge, leaves the car there, and catches a train to god-knows-where.

Petit's admiration for German minimalist Wim Wenders extends not only to having him as associate producer, but also to casting Lisa Kreuzer as his female lead. Kreuzer played in KINGS OF THE ROAD, a similarly bleak road movie, and was the girl looking for Alice in Wender's ALICE IN THE CITIES. The child she searches for in RADIO ON is also called Alice, one of several devices probably intended to enamour the film to German audiences, the other being the extensive, untranslated German dialogue. (The film was co-produced by a German company).

Shot in black and white, RADIO ON is one long splurge of dullness relieved only by in-jokes and references comprehensible to cineastes of a Marxist persuasion. (Viz. Robert's flat is over a cinema playing Oshiwa's EMPIRE OF PASSION, he has several t.v. sets playing simultaneously in his living room, which is painted flat and white like a prison, the dead boy's flat is decorated with the famous, if highly pretentious poster proclaiming the links between Fritz Lang, Werner Von Braun and electronic reality of the 'eighties, etc, etc.) The photography is drab and the car's departure from London follows an incomprehensible route designed to show as many high-rise flats and gas-works as possible, a type of work Ealing Studios accomplished far more efficiently 30 years ago. Robert strikes us as either a ruinously uninteresting, soulless young man, or the sort of mild-mannered nutter who could turn on you at a moment's notice. But he doesn't yield one spark of gumption and quickly turns out to be such an unsympathetic hero that our interest in his quest rapidly dissolves.

RADIO ON's use of contemporary rock music, largely of the synthesised German variety of course, is fairly deft but very self-conscious. The musical images swing between the simple iconoclasm of the 'fifties and 'sixties, and the cold, anaesthetic isolation of today. Robert's car stereo has a cassette to orchestrate every metaphor in Petit's script!

This was Petit's first film and although boring and depressing, RADIO ON shows a tenacity of purpose that is already starting to bear fruit in his latest film AN UNSUITABLE JOB FOR A WOMAN. The main trouble with RADIO ON is that it *had* no purpose.

Britain   1979   102 mins
Dir: Christopher Petit   *Prod:* Keith Griffiths
Prod. Co: British Film Institute/Road Movies Filmproduktion (Berlin)
Script: Christopher Petit
Cast incl: David Beams, Lisa Kreuzer, Sue Jones-Davies, Sting, Andrew Byatt, Sandy Ratcliff, Sabina Michael and Katja Kersten

THE RAIN PEOPLE

Well on his way to becoming the unsung hero of the road movie, James Caan's second crack at the genre was in this curious little item directed by Francis Ford Coppola, shortly before they both went on to better things with THE GODFATHER. In THE RAIN PEOPLE Caan plays Kilgannon, a brain-damaged victim of college football who's now trying to find a job in the real world. He's picked up by Natalie, who is running away from a stifling marriage. Kilgannon is just the charity case that she's been looking for in order to give her life some meaning, and she's determined to help him restore his dignity. Of course she has to take things one step at a time, which is why she settles for a job at a road-side reptile farm. After having settled him in there, she's wracked with the neurotic fear of over-indulging the boy, decides to leave him pronto, and in her haste gets booked for speeding. The local judge turns out to be the money-grabbing snake-breeder, and he somehow manages to take Kilgannon's $1000 college pension in respect of Natalie's fine. After that THE RAIN PEOPLE becomes inordinately complicated, with writer/director Coppola trying to turn the whole thing into a psycho drama that neither the actors nor the story really need.

Still, up until Natalie's arrest, this is an eminently watchable road movie with attractive shots of the Colorado scenery, rain splattered windscreens and complimentary performances from the featured players.

USA   1969   101 mins
Dir: Francis Ford Coppola   *Prod:* Bart Patton and Ronald Colby
Prod. Co: Coppola Co.   *Script:* Coppola
Cast incl: James Caan, Shirley Knight, Robert Duvall, Marya Zimmet, Tom Aldredge, Laurie Crews and Andrew Duncan

THE REBEL ROUSERS

This film is so rare that it hardly even shows up in most biographies of its two stars, Jack Nicholson and Bruce Dern. This is possibly because THE REBEL ROUSERS is such an awful piece of work that powerful forces in Hollywood have done their best to bury it in deference to the actors' current reputations. The story is an unremarkable outlaw gang chase involving B-road regulars Dianna Ladd and Cameron Mitchell, but it's certainly no worse than other biker pics both stars made in their infancy.

USA	1969	81 mins
Dir: Martin B. Cohen		*Prod:* n/a
Prod. Co: Paragon Intl.		*Script:* n/a
Cast incl: Jack Nicholson, Bruce Dern, Cameron Mitchell and Dianna Ladd		

RED BALL EXPRESS

The title RED BALL EXPRESS refers to the high speed, non-stop trucking system that kept supplies moving to the front in war-time France. The film imposes a story of racial prejudice and sadistic officers onto this basic storyline, and it doesn't really work. Uncertain direction from Budd Boetticher and a lack-lustre cast fail to distinguish the work from myriad second division service movies.

USA	1952	Length: n/a
Dir: Budd Boetticher		*Prod:* Aaron Rosenberg
Prod. Co: Universal		*Script:* John Michael Hayes
Cast incl: Jeff Chandler, Alex Nicol, Charles Drake, Hugh O'Brian, Frank Chase, Jack Kelly, Cindy Garner and Judith Braun		

JEFF CHANDLER · ALEX NICOL
Judith Braun · Charles Drake
in **THE RED BALL EXPRESS** (U)
A Universal-International Picture   G.F.D. Release

RED LINE 7000

Having already laid the ground rules in 1932 with THE CROWD ROARS, Howard Hawks returned to motor racing movies in 1965 with RED LINE 7000. However, rather than revive his own formula (Cornell Wilde had already done that with DRIVE A CROOKED ROAD) RED LINE 7000 owes more to the sort of loose-knit social spiders' webs of Robert Altman. George Kirkgo's screenplay, written from Hawks' own story, introduces us to several stockcar racers, and in the process of establishing their identities, delineates the rivalries and dependencies that are the film's *raison d'etre*, if not its actual plot. There is, of course, a racing climax which thrives on the tensions and frailties created earlier.

In another complete contrast to ROARS, Hawks used a cast of largely unknown actors to play in his motley circus of stockcar addicts, including a youthful James Caan as a crippled driver and Charlene Holt, who plays a girl convinced that she's the jinx that's killed several racers... much hand-wringing in *that* performance, of course. For one of the last films made before he died, Hawks naturally surrounded himself with the expertise that a director of his stature attracted. The pay-off is some excellent photography and slick, even flashy editing. The actors tend towards the method school style of delivery that was fashionable in live theatre at the time, there being a lot of stuttering and stumbling over lines and gestures in the dialogue. This supports my belief that although in his dotage, Hawks was dabbling in new forms of movie making, but without having any great confidence in them.

USA   1965   105 mins
Dir: Howard Hawks   *Prod:* Hawks
Prod. Co: Paramount   *Script:* George Kirkgo
Cast incl: James Caan, Charlene Holt, Laura Devon, Gail Hire, John
Robert Crawford, James Ward and Norman Alden

ROAD GAMES

Not before time, I suppose, a road movie from that *other* country where travel has helped shape the social character and the commerce of a young and restless nation. However, although ROAD GAMES is an Australian film, it stars two excellent American actors: Stacey Keach as an eccentric trucker, who spouts poetry to his largely disinterested dog, and Jamie Lee Curtis as a hitch-hiking heiress (shades of Ali MacGraw in CONVOY). Keach's fantasies about the lives of other road users are interrupted by radio bulletins reporting a series of murders that seem to be following him on his 2000 mile trip from Melbourne to Perth. Incidental clues along the way make Keach suspicious of a sinister black van and its driver, but neither the police nor anyone else will listen to him. After Jamie Lee disappears in the vicinity of the van, Keach is resolved to catch its driver, who he's now convinced is the murderer. The tension that's hitherto been fractured by Keach's sardonic ramblings and his badinage with Jamie Lee, now gels and elevates the rest of the story to a sort of Brian De Palma-cum-Alfred Hitchcock chase. Keach's cargo of frozen pork and some well-staged double-entendres provide the necessary shock value, and Keach's missionary zeal is well tempered by an understandable fear. However, Everett DeRoche's script suddenly falls apart toward the very end of the story, as if he couldn't conceive of how Keach would react if he finally met his quarry.

Although ROAD GAMES isn't a tour-de-force thriller like DUEL or WAGES OF FEAR, it's far superior to low-budget U.S. road movies of its ilk. Director Richard Franklin isn't quite yet in the same class as Australian peers like Peter Weir and Bruce Beresford, but he makes the most of a simple plot and, with Vincent Monton, he ably contrasts the vulnerability of Stacy Keach, Jamie Lee and the truck, with the raw power of the Australian landscape. It certainly makes a change from Arizona!

AUSTRALIA   1981   100 mins
Dir: Richard Franklin   *Prod:* Franklin
Prod. Co: Quest   *Script:* Everett DeRoche
Cast incl: Stacy Keach, Jamie Lee Curtis, Marion Edward, Grant Page, Bill Stacey and Thaddeus Smith

---

ROAD MOVIE

By using the name of the genre as the title for his film, Joseph Strick set himself up for the most meticulous scrutiny, if not actual ridicule. But presumably he felt that he could afford such a conceit after drawing boundless accolades for his direction of THE SAVAGE EYE, ULYSSES and TROPIC OF CANCER. Four years passed between the release of CANCER and the completion of ROAD MOVIE, and there's much evidence in the latter to suggest that he spent the time ensuring that his new film would have maximum impact. ROAD MOVIE is therefore a finely detailed and scrupulously constructed film, but its abiding sense of bitterness and despair blinded many critics to its excellence – both as an exercise in movie-making, and as an entertainment in its own right... not that the two should be mutually exclusive, of course.

There's not really much of a story to ROAD MOVIE. It gets underway by slowly creating an impression of the trucking life, as seen through the eyes of indie drivers, Gil (Robert Drivas) and Hank (Barry Bostwick). The big hauliers try and squeeze them out of business, a process encouraged by their two bankers and the restrictive legislation of governments and unions. Suddenly Dame Fate arrives, in the unlikely shape of an itinerant prostitute, Janice (Regina Baff), who has the engaging habit of keeping her money in her wig, and offers the boys a good time in return for a lift to New York. Gil and Hank, cynical though they are, take up the deal with a kind of philosophical compliance, although they soon realise their error of judgement. At the end of her useful life as a hooker, this spiritually beaten, physically drained individual symbolises the mean backlash of emancipation. She craves affection, but her abrasive manner prevents her from getting any, even from men as desperate as herself. And so when she realises that she's never going to be anything more than a sex object, even to Gil and Hank, she's moved to punish them for not delivering. The effects of this are quite literally catastrophic, with Strick and scriptwriter Judith Rascoe going, perhaps, a little too far in making the point that hell hath no fury like a woman scorned.

Strick's choice of the grim consequence over the satisfactory resolution is justified by every other element of the film. Each human gesture is a pessimistic statement, each line of the screenplay an expression of defeat, and it's all set amongst a scenario of destitution and bleakness. For Strick's vision of America as mankind's trashcan depicts freeways running through industrial wastelands; polluted landscapes relieved only by dirty, inhospitable truckstops and tract housing and is altogether as gloomy as the perception his main charcters have of themselves.

It is difficult to watch the film without feeling profoundly dismal, a sensation not helped by the strong thread of misogyny that runs through it, justifying as it does many of Janice's nastier traits. But ROAD MOVIE was written by a woman, and tries valiantly in its 88 minutes to explore more lucidly the inner turmoil of a woman stuck on the down escalator. Strick himself came from a trucking family, so one can't question his understanding of the haulage business, but his insistence on the darker side of reality is perhaps too laboured and ends up as its own cliché, much like the tinkling, homely country'n'western music that orchestrates it.

The acting in ROAD MOVIE never holds Strick back from his goal. Drivas

and Bostwick, two television players who have turned their hands to most things on the small screen, correctly underplay the pair of male chauvinists out of their depth in business and emotional maturity. But it's Miss Baff who is the star of this film. Like Gil and Hank, she can't adequately explain her dehumanised feelings, but in her almost involuntary tantrums and bitchiness, she becomes an inarticulate spokeswoman for women's lib. Like Minnie Mouse on amphetemines, she stomps through ROAD MOVIE with a relentless angst and it's quite amazing that her two hosts survive as long as they do. Perhaps its not so surprising that audiences found her only slightly less hard to take than they did Strick's observations of America's countryside. The film did poorly at the box office but, I feel sure, will be recognised for its excellence in the fullness of time.

USA   1974   88 mins.
Dir: Joseph Strick   *Prod:* Strick
Prod. Co: Grove Press Films   *Script:* Judith Rascoe
Photog: Don Lenzer
Cast incl: Gil – Robert Drivas; Hank – Barry Bostwick; Janice – Regina
             Baff; Harry – David Bauer

RUN ANGEL, RUN

The fourth of producer Joe Solomon's biker quickies (with THE LOSERS still to come), RUN ANGEL, RUN marked the directorial debut of Jack Starrett, and featured his sister Jennifer and wife Valerie just to keep it cosy.

Once again it's a chase flick, with a burly William Smith on the run from the biker gang he "exposed" to a sensation-hungry magazine, for a fast $10,000. Really! Along the way, Smith picks up Mrs. Starrett, playing the obligatory topless-dancer-cum-hooker and they rather uneasily (and unconvincingly) set up house together whilst waiting for the money to come through. Unfortunately for them, the daughter of the magazine's editor, played far too gracefully by ballet dancer Margaret Markov, is raped by members of the vengeance seeking outlaws, and she leads them to the house where Smith and Starrett are struggling with a less than blissful domesticity. Carnage ensues.

Editor Renn Reynolds copped the flash-forward techniques developed by Dennis Hopper in EASY RIDER, and occasional bursts of multi-screening make the most of John Stephens' okay camerawork. But no amount of icing can turn this bread and butter into cake, and it remains pretty hard to digest. Starrett should have stuck to acting.

USA   1969   95 mins
Dir: Jack Starrett   *Prod:* Joe Solomon
Prod. Co: Fanfare   *Script:* Jerome Wish and V. A. Furlong
Cast incl: Williams Smith, Valerie Starrett, Gene Shane, Lee De Broux, Paul Harper and Jennifer Starrett

SILVER DREAM RACER

I'm afraid I have a pathological inability to take David Essex seriously, either as an actor or a pop singer. The two talents are not as similar as popular wisdom or inflamed egos would suppose and, even in those rare cases where these disparate abilities reside in one body, few 20th century heros have managed to dovetail their two careers successfully. On balance, I think Essex is probably a slightly better actor than he is a pop singer, and SILVER DREAM RACER seems to be a fairly serious attempt on his part to prove it (i.e. he doesn't keep bursting into song every ten minutes... although there is a grim, Essex-sung title song).

The storyline is utterly formula: Essex as the shoe-string amateur bikeracer, Beau Bridges as the snotty champ with a reputation for foul play on the track and caddish behaviour off it. Fortunes shuffle when Essex's brother is killed in a trail-bike accident (possibly a world first!), and he acquires the dead man's pet project, the lovingly built "siver dream" bike of the film's title. Bridge's girlfriend, played by Christina Raines, turns out to be the ex– of another racer Bridges is rumoured to have forced into a fatal accident, and her allegiances are thus as slippery as gearbox oil. I don't think you need any hints as to the outcome of all this but I will say that script and direction, both by David Wickes, elevate efficiency dangerously close to an art form.

Wickes has a solid grounding in t.v. crime drama and hit the big screen with a spin-off from one of the most popular of these, SWEENEY ONE. He wisely asks as little as possible of his main characters and manages to keep things moving at a fair old tilt without opting for the easy route and losing the story in a welter of racing footage. The relationships between Essex and his family, employer (a nicely sour cameo from the late Harry H. Corbett) and the other two stars are given their due, and whenever Essex's awkwardly cute mannerisms run the risk of raising hackles, he deftly cuts to another scene.

And Wickes nearly pulls it off. But he is not a Norman Taurog or a Richard Thorpe nor does he have their advantage of working with a mega-star like Elvis Presley who, though no great actor, at least had flair and charisma going for him. SILVER DREAM RACER is, then, a better crafted film than SPEEDWAY or FUN IN ACUPULCO, but not a more entertaining one. And the onus for that rests squarely with David Essex.

Great Britain	1980	111 mins
Dir: David Wickes		*Prod:* René Dupont
Prod. Co: Rank		*Script:* Wickes

Cast incl: David Essex, Beau Bridges, Cristina Raines, Clarke Peters, Harry H. Corbett, Diane Keen, Lee Montague and Patrick Ryecart

SLITHER

A first-time shot by Howard Zieff, who made his name directing witty, good-looking t.v. commercials, SLITHER surprises no-one by being a witty, good-looking road movie. For the latter, we can once again thank Laszlo Kovacs, and for the humour, producer Jack Sher bought an astringently funny first script by W.D. Richter. The equally inspired cast of ascending stars is headed by James Caan as paroled car thief, Dick Kanipsia, who is told by a dying embezzler, Harry Moss (Richard Shull), of riches beyond his wildest dreams that await him if he contacts one Barry Feneka (Peter Boyle). Feneka is Moss's ex-partner who has patiently bided his time as a rather awful nightclub comedian until Moss showed up to go after the loot with him. En route to the small Californian town where he lives with his terminally naive wife, Louise Lasser, Caan hitches a lift with a babbling speedfreak, Kitty (Sally Kellerman). Their reception at Chez Moss is coloured with a fine cynicism, but Moss eventually represses most of his mistrust and agrees to go along with Kanipsia to "investment counsellor", Harry Palmer (Allen Garfield), who apparently has the $300,000 they're after. Their quest involves an unlikely mixture of mystery, violence and high comedy with Palmer himself.

For starters, Boyle insists on making the trip in a huge station-wagon with his wife and a caravan trailer in tow – the antithesis of the svelte transports normally involved in road movies. Then there's a pair of ominous black vans that shadow them during their journey and their cargo of sinister businessmen – or are they really hit-men? Kanipsia is alternately threatened and re-assured by everything and everyone in SLITHER, especially Kitty and Barry Fenaka and Caan's interpretation of the man is well measured, although a little too diffident in parts.

Garfield as the bumbling money-man, Boyle and Louise Lasser (playing virtually the same confused housewife of television's MARY HARTMAN, MARY HARTMAN), are in fact the film's strongest assets. Watching them cope with a fight in Boyle's trailer park bingo hall is to witness a masterpiece of comic juxtaposition and understatement, for the film rests more on stray expressions and movements than it does on the contrivances of its script.

Not a great movie by the standards of this or probably any other critic, SLITHER nevertheless demands repeated viewing... each time you see it, new delights manifest themselves, whilst the production quality and visual gleam maintain their initial impact.

USA	1973	96 mins
Dir: Howard Zieff		*Prod:* Jack Sher
Prod. Co: MGM		*Script:* W. D. Richter

Cast incl: James Caan, Sally Kellerman, James Garfield, Peter Boyle, Louise Lasser and Richard B. Shull

SPEEDWAY

As pure cinema, most of Elvis Presley's films were pretty awful and conceived mainly as promotional devices to flog albums, soundtrack and otherwise. SPEEDWAY doesn't even come close to breaking the mould.

Presley plays a successful racing driver who is being chased by smarty-pants Nancy Sinatra (having cleaned up her WILD ANGELS image). She turns out to be a tax inspector and he turns out to owe $145,000, largely due to his manager's penchant for gambling away the Presley spoils. Mr. Presley is not too happy about this state of affairs, but since he'd already decided that Nancy was his kinda girl, he decides to do the honourable thing, win the Big Race, pay the tax with the proceeds and kiss her a lot. His plans go awry when he crashes badly during practice, but everyone chips in and helps him rebuild his car in time for the race. In a rare example of the downbeat, Philip Shuken's script doesn't actually let Presley win. He does, of course, win enough lap money to pay off most of the debt.

Despite this unlikely denouement, SPEEDWAY is the usual collection of squeaky-clean romance, mediocre songs and back-projection. Only worth seeing if you've still got blue suede shoes.

USA   1968   94 mins
Dir: Norman Taurog   *Prod:* Douglas Laurence
Prod. Co: MGM   *Script:* Phillip Shuken
Cast incl: Elvis Presley, Nancy Sinatra, Bill Bixby, Gale Gordon, William
          Schallert, Ross Hagen, Carl Ballantine and Harry Hickox

STEEL ARENA

Preceding his excellent TRUCKSTOP WOMAN by just one year, STEEL ARENA concerns itself with the rise of Dusty Russell from demolition derby champ to auto dare devil, i.e. propelling himself 100 feet through the air in a beat-up auto. To bring the film in on a $150,000 budget, Lester used the real stuntmen from Russell's own Circus of Death, a travelling show that played the showgrounds of the mid-west. With Russell playing himself and an assortment of picaresque characters such as the man who blows himself up in a coffin, and a Circus of Death groupie, STEEL ARENA has a distinct documentary quality to it. But Lester makes it work as entertainment in a wider context by gently sending up everyone concerned, whilst still according them the respect their dangerous profession deserves. Waggish editing and clever musical clues are a means to this end, which leaves the cast to speak for themselves, quite literally in fact, for much of the dialogue appears to have been made up on the spot.

Although it frequently reveals its rough edges, STEEL ARENA is an absorbing, generously spirited film which should not be missed. (Lester's only previous work was TRICIA'S WEDDING, an outlandish spoof of the Nixon nuptuals by the transvestite Cockettes.)

USA   1973   98 mins.
Dir: Mark L. Lester   *Prod:* Peter Traynor and Lester
Prod. Co: n/a   *Script:* Lester
Cast incl: Dusty Russell, Gene Drew, Buddy Love, Speed Sterns, Ed
          'Chromedome' Ryan, Laura Books, Nancy Walton and Eric
          Nord

THE SORCERER

Its misleading title applied presumably to cash in on his success with THE EXORCIST, William Friedkin's THE SORCERER is in fact a bloated re-make of H.G. Clouzot's classic trucking film, WAGES OF FEAR.

In a superhuman and utterly superfluous effort to distinguish his work from the original, Friedkin and scriptwriter Walon Green add an hour's worth of prologue to the story of four desperate men hauling gelignite through horrible adversity. This establishes, by virtue of expensive location shooting in Paris, Mexico, Israel and America, how the four came to meet up in an unnamed Latin American backwater. The remainder of the film traces Clouzot's original script fairly pedantically, with an international cast ensuring THE SORCERER's commerciality in foreign markets, if not adding any real social tension to the proceedings.

Roy Scheider, as the American low-lifer, Scanlon, exudes just about enough reckless determination, and is at least identifiable to English speaking audiences who saw THE FRENCH CONNECTION. One performance is not a good enough reason to spend 122 minutes watching this farrago of misguided intention, however.

USA	1978	122 mins.
Dir: William Friedkin		*Prod:* Friedkin
Prod. Co: Paramount/Universal		*Script:* Walon Green

Cast incl: Roy Scheider, Bruno Cremer, Francisco Rabel, Amidou, Ramon Bieri, Pater Capell, Karl John and Frederick Ledebur

STINGRAY

Another t.v. director turns his career toward the big screen and gets carried away with the possibilities that open up to him. Or rather, in the case of Richard Taylor and STINGRAY, the director wanted to try and do everything himself.

It's a routine juvenile chase film with juvenile actors working from Taylor's juvenile script. Christopher Mitchum (Robert's son) plays one half of a teenage double act who finally acquire their dream car, a 1962 Chevvy Stingray. The trouble is, that a drug ring have stashed large quantities of money and heroin in its trunk and, not surprisingly, they'd like to get it all back. Stunts a'go-go ensue, with Mitchum and his pal, Les Lannom, involved in cross country motorcycle chases, several shoot-outs and a halfway decent bar brawl. But Taylor's mistake in all this is that he's far too busy looking through the lens and chaperoning his young wards to wield the knife. His editing, to say the least, is undisciplined.

And then there's his squandering of the film's most interesting character, the female gang leader played by Sherry Jackson. She's a laconic little hussy with a tremendous line in sour-mouthed reprimand and an eager left-hook, both of which she regularly applies to her dithering henchmen (Bill Watson and Bert Hinchman). Taylor doesn't use her enough, and the two kids in the Chevvy are mere amateurs by comparison. So, I'm afraid, is the film.

USA   1978   99 mins.
Dir: Richard Taylor   *Prod:* Donald Ham and Bill Bruce
Prod. Co: Avco Embassy   *Script:* Taylor
Cast incl: Christopher Mitchum, Les Lannom, Sherry Jackson, Bill Watson, Bert Hinchman, Cliff Emmich, Sondra Theodore

SUGARLAND EXPRESS

Loosely based on the true story of Bobby and Ila Faye Dent and their flight from the Texas State Police in 1969, THE SUGARLAND EXPRESS is a magnificently divulged testimony to the noble loser. It was also Steven Spielberg's second road movie, made whilst he was still in the tenure of Universal Studios, but without the financial constraints of his first, the highly profitable DUEL. Between them, DUEL and SUGARLAND EXPRESS provide benchmark examples of the highway chase, that most ubiquitous of road movie sub-strata. But working with the confidence of experience and success, plus the full backing of Richard D. Zanuck in his heyday at Universal, Spielberg created a commercial classic out of SUGARLAND, whereas DUEL never made it beyond being a cult favourite.

Having herself been recently freed from a short prison sentence, Lou Jean Poplin (Goldie Hawn) visits her husband Clovis (Bill Atherton), in a Texas pre-release facility. She tells him that welfare authorities have taken away their baby, Langsten, and are planning to have him adopted by a family in the town of Sugarland. Although he's about to be paroled, Lou Jean persuades the extremely reluctant Clovis that if he doesn't escape and help her get the child back right away, they'll never see him again. Lou Jean manages to smuggle Clovis away from the prison in a car driven by a Mr. Nocker, but when he is stopped by a patrolman for driving with "excessive caution", the Poplins find themselves obliged to abduct the officer in his own car. Patrolman Maxwell Slide (Michael Sacks) is initially fearful of Clovis and his feigned willingness to shoot him with his own revolver if he doesn't do exactly as they say. But after Clovis has used this threat to get them through a couple of police roadblocks, Slide becomes privy to the nervous, almost adolescent banter between his two kidnappers. He realises that for them this is a mercy dash; and it dawns on him that the only real danger he's in is with his boss, Capt. Tanner, for letting this happen in the first place. Tanner (Ben Johnson) feels the same way about the Poplins, as he's been listening to most of Slide's progress over the police radio. Although he doubts Clovis intends to use the gun, he takes the path of least resistance and allows the police-car to continue on its route to Sugarland, followed at a sensible distance by his own patrolmen. However, local police forces and the media hear about the Clovis' saga over the police wavebands, and soon the procession is swollen by over two hundred patrolcars, t.v. and radio trucks and sightseers. Tanner's concern for the Poplins extends to him arresting two reserve deputies who unsuccessfully ambush the pair whilst they're spending the night in a trailer parked in a used car lot. And Slide's compassion for Lou Jean and Clovis has developed into an affinity based on a recognition of the naiveties and doubts he sees reflected in himself. Lou Jean feels this herself when she remarks wistfully: "If baby Langsten were here now, we'd be a real family."

However, when they are in the final approaches to Sugarland, the early tension of their journey returns as Tanner plays it safe and orders a squad of marksmen to wait in readiness for any false move Clovis might make with the gun. As they close in on the house where baby Langsten is being kept, Slide senses that a trap has been sprung and tries to make Clovis drive on past. But Lou Jean is desperate to get her child back and forces the car to stop. In the confusion that follows, Clovis is shot and killed.

His death hits us like a rabbit punch. Spielberg has pieced together an aura of invincibility around the Poplins, based on the rightness of the cause, rather than the cunning or brute force that's elemental to many a chase movie. Even a tough old cop like Tanner is disarmed by the sight of Lou Jean bubbling with delight as she steals armfuls of her favourite trading stamps when they stop for gas. In more intimate moments we share her concern about hair-do and make up as she primps for a t.v. camera crew, we watch her badger Clovis into stopping the car for a picnic, and we see the three of them exchanging jokes, personal snap-shots and glib homilies as if they were on some camping trip. This picture of adolescents trapped in adult bodies explains the simplistic reactions Lou Jean, Clovis and Slide offer to the greater challenges around them, too. The script, by Hal Barwood and Mathew Robbins, idly suggests that the responsibility for their stunted maturity lies somewhere in the fast-food, t.v. quiz-game society they live in. This fits in with the instant celebrity status accorded them by the media, its jokiness emphasised by Spielberg's aerial longshots looking back at the vast cortege following the patrolcar; but it's easy, I think, to find this all a little too flip. The Poplins are anomalies, and before we allow ourselves to become too beguiled by their strangeness and innocence, or condemn the world that made them, we are jogged back to the fact that this is a seriously mounted chase. There are no nursery rhymes played on the police radio, but there's plenty of thudding bodywork, usually when over-zealous police cars collide with each other, and enough gunfire to satisfy most people. Although Spielberg never throws in anything to excess, what he does use, he maximises.

"When a bullet punctures glass in SUGARLAND EXPRESS," he explained, "not only does the glass spiderweb, but the entire windshield is torn loose from its nuts and holders and goes flying across the lot. And when a tyre is hit by a bullet, the whole tyre blows up, the hubcap flies off, and the entire car settles in a plume of dust. I really wanted to make this violent pyrotechnically; I wanted you to feel that the flying glass could do just as much harm to the characters as the actual velocity of the screaming bullets."

The performances in SUGARLAND EXPRESS are less exaggerated than the special effects, although there is perhaps a little initial resistance to Goldie Hawn pushing the spectre of LAUGH IN's zany comedienne into what must be judged as a rather different role. But then the character of Lou Jean Poplin is really nothing more than a Texan cliche; an ex-waitress or typist escaped from the drudge of wage-earning and bum-pinching to investigate what lay beyond the cornbelt, but who somehow never made it. Her foibles and silly preoccupations are really not that much different from our own, and her greater mission – to retrieve her son – is completely identifiable. We start off feeling mildly infuriated by Goldie Hawn as Lou Jean, but end up enamoured of an eccentricity that might have blossomed into a Myrna Loy or Katherine Hepburn character if it wasn't for the fetters of her culture.

Maxwell and Clovis are sterner prospects. Both characters were involved in the caper against their better judgements, their underlying innocence masked throughout by a kind of clumsy pragmatism. Both men are also softened by feelings that are new and slightly foreign to them: Clovis' paternal instincts assume a greater dimension as he gets deeper and deeper into his mission; Maxwell Slide experiences something approaching kinship with the Poplins, admiring and empathising with their simple, if cockeyed morality. There was even a close physical resemblance between Michael Sacks (Slide) and William Atherton (Clovis), which Spielberg claims was intentional:

"They were deliberately cast to resemble one another – if not closely in body, then at least in spirit and attitude. We wanted two actors cut from the same cloth, two characters who could have lived in the same neighbourhood, grown up together, and then gone their separate ways – one into the police force and the other into holy wedlock with an irresponsible blonde bombshell."

What's so special about each of the characters is that they unfold and catalyse in the confinement of the car. Almost all the dialogue takes place there, and yet there's no sense of claustrophobia, and only an occasional need to interrupt their developing relationship – which inevitably must include Tanner, via the car radio – by stopping and looking for external diversions. Spielberg, his cast and cameraman Vilmos Zsigmond, by their craft and ingenuity, have avoided this traditional pitfall of the road movie.

"Because it was such a monumental logistical problem," concurs Spielberg, "everything in THE SUGARLAND EXPRESS was worked out beforehand on a highly detailed master screenplay. In fact it was worked out to the point where the prose was so metaphorical that it inspired a lot of shots in the movie.

"You have to know (scriptwriters) Barwood and Robbins' work to understand what I mean, but for instance, they described in one shot five police cars zooming past the camera like the Daytona 500 – which immediately brings to mind the titled camera image that you're so used to seeing on the 'Wide World of Sports at the Daytona 500'. That kind of metaphor, that kind of imagery contained in a simple sentence helped trigger half of the shots to mind.

"I had a graphic artist come into my office and sketch the entire movie on what you could call a Shell Oil map which I was able to tape on one wall of my hotel room in Texas. So I could see exactly what the film would look like from a bird's eye view as it progressed from one police car followed by two, then ten, then fifty, plus all the pit stops throughout the movie. So I always had a visual overview in terms of day to day scheduling.

"But there's a danger in being so thoroughly prepared that when you come

on the set the next day your thinking is not spontaneous because it doesn't fit into the homework pattern of the night before. Marvellous accidents happen on the set – actors have suggestions, technicians have suggestions, a passing stranger might have a suggestion – and I think a director should keep his mind open everyday and not get trapped by the kind of homework he falls in love with on the eve of shooting the actual scene."

Spielberg's easy embrace of technology, meticulous preparation and casual influence works better for DUEL and SUGARLAND than it does for his later, more complex films. The satisfying balance of script, acting and direction in SUGARLAND EXPRESS establishes the film as a bridge between Spielberg's early television work (DUEL was originally made for the tube) and his grandiose accomplishments with JAWS and CLOSE ENCOUNTERS. What it shares with the later films is an understanding of unassuming, unimportant Americans dealing instinctively with situations that all but overwhelm them. This is why they are so appealing to mass audiences, and why SUGARLAND's native kookiness should not blind you to its excellence as a piece of movie-making.

USA   1974   110 mins.
Dir: Steven Spielberg   *Prod:* Richard D. Zanuck and David Brown
Prod. Co: Universal   *Script:* Hal Barwood and Matthew Robbins
Photog: Vilmos Zsigmond   *Stunt Dir:* Cary Loftin
Cast incl: Lou Jean Poplin – Goldie Hawn; Clovis Poplin – William Atherton; Maxwell Slide – Michael Sacks; Capt. Tanner – Ben Johnson. Also featuring: Dean Smith, Ted Grossman, Harrison Zanuck, Gene Rader and Kenneth Crone

TEN DAYS TO TULARA

Lightweight, true-grit meller based around Sterling Hayden's efforts to recover his kidnapped son in Central America. Native rituals, stolen bullion shipments and a daring-ish aircraft escape feature in this below average support feature; abundant talent and credible scripting do not.

USA   1958   77 mins.
Dir: George Sherman   *Prod:* Sherman and Clarence Eurist
Prod. Co: Sherman/Eurist   *Script:* Laurence Mascott
Cast incl: Sterling Hayden, Grace Raynor, Rodolfo Hoyos, Juan Garcia, Carlos Muzquiz and Felix Gonzales

THIEVES' HIGHWAY

A film which relies on archetypal Italian histrionics for dramatic effect is never easy to watch, but THIEVES' HIGHWAY is thankfully quite a short production, and leading actress Valentina Cortese supplants the usual Mediterranean posturing with a sturdy veneer of guile and coherency. She plays the moll hired by crooked San Francisco produce dealer, Figlia (Lee J. Cobb), to divert truck driver Nick Garcos (Richard Conte) from his efforts to nail Figlia for causing an accident that crippled his father. Conte's vocation and Figlia's business allow for lots of trucking action and colourful intrigue, all of it well photographed and making maximum use of the impressive North California coastal region. Although the bad girl with the heart of gold and the son avenging the suffering of his dad are ancient plot gambits, we must remember that this *is* an old film. THIEVES' HIGHWAY nevertheless has a confidence and a seamless execution that does its director, Jules Dassin, some considerable credit. If only there weren't so many American actors trying to ape the most irritating traits of the Italian national.

USA   1949   94 mins.
Dir: Jules Dassin   *Prod:* Robert Bassler
Prod. Co: 20th Century Fox   *Script:* A.L. Bezzerides
Cast incl: Richard Conte, Valentina Cortese, Lee J. Cobb, Jack Oakie,
Barbara Lawrence, Millard Mitchell and Joseph Pevney

THIEVES LIKE US

Unlike most Altman films, THIEVES LIKE US has the form and content of conventional melodrama, although there are the usual humorous gaffes undermining what could have been effective dramatic statements. This is a trait that annoys many Altman critics and another one, thankfully limited to this film and THE LONG GOODBYE, is the abundance of Coca-Cola recepticles that litter the footage – cans in GOODBYE, bottles in THIEVES. Is this a running in-joke for Hollywood decadents, or were these two pics financed by the beverage manufacturer?

The story treads fairly obviously in the footsteps of Arthur Penn's BONNIE AND CLYDE: Bowie (Keith Carradine), a young murderer, T-Dub (Bert Ramsen), an ageing bank robber, and Chicamaw (John Shuck), a part-Indian ruffian, escape from their Mississippi prison farm and start robbing banks. This is the time of the Great Depression of course, and it's debatable whether it's the popular press or their own egos which are most anxious to mythologise a successor to the Clyde Barrow Gang. But this shambling trio, soon joined by Bowie's girlfriend (Shelley Duvall looking more the flat-faced waif than ever before or since) are hardly up to the job... especially when T-Dub, the alleged professional on the team, gets smitten by a frowsy beautician (Louise Fletcher).

THIEVES LIKE US isn't as richly laden with 'thirties imagery and ephemera as BONNIE AND CLYDE or PAPER MOON, as Altman relies more on incidental radio broadcasts to set the period (e.g. an episode of 'The Gangbusters' plays with a nice sense of irony as they amateurishly plan a bank robbery, a dramatisation of 'Romeo

and Juliet' accompanies Duvall and Carradine as they cumbersomely attempt to make love for the first time).

The performances are always competent and in the cases of Shuck and Carradine, excellent. But the script appears to have had an inherent theatricality that the actors don't fully bring to the screen. Maybe Altman's fledgling repertory company were having such fun together, revelling in their cloistered camaradie, that they forsook the demands and potential of the story.

USA   1973   123 mins.
Dir: Robert Altman   *Prod:* Jerry Brick
Prod. Co: United Artists   *Script:* Joan Tewkesbury, Calder Willingham
                                        and Altman
Cast incl: Keith Carradine, Shelley Duvall, John Shuck, Bert Ramsen,
        Louise Fletcher, Ann Latham and Tom Skerritt.

THEN CAME BRONSON

Sub-EASY RIDER twaddle starring Michael Parks, who somehow managed to help turn it into a t.v. series, and a modified Harley-Davidson Sportster that performs almost as intuitively as any of the actors in the film (except perhaps Martin Sheen).

James Bronson (Parks) is a disillusioned young writer – aren't we all? – who, after an argument with his newspaper editor, sets off on a trek to Find Himself... if not America. Much of the script concerns itself with the vacuous relationship between Bronson and a wilfully 'mysterious' girl who has just been jilted (Bonnie Bedelia). Their dialogue is as pointless as THEN CAME BRONSON's purpose, and nothing in the direction or photography compensates for that.

USA   1970   98 mins.
Dir: William A. Graham   *Prod:* Robert H. Justman
Prod. Co: EMI   *Script:* D.B. Petticlerc
Cast incl: Michael Parks, Bonnie Bedelia, Akim Tamiroff, Gary Merrill,
        Sheree North and Martin Sheen

THEY DRIVE BY NIGHT

Like many of the great directors, Raoul Walsh shifted effortlessly between genres, and although best known for his westerns and gangster thrillers, his one stab at road movies is on a par with anything else he's done. The only exception I can think of, in fact, is the film he made with Humphrey Bogart immediately after THEY DRIVE BY NIGHT, also in 1940: HIGH SIERRA.

Rather like ROAD MOVIE, Walsh and his scriptwriters, Jerry Wald and Richard Macaulay, spend the first half of THEY DRIVE BY NIGHT creating a realistic (for the time) image of the trucking business. George Raft and Bogart play Joe and Paul Fabrini, a pair of indies working too hard, skimping on things where they can, but boisterously optimistic nonetheless. However, their spirits are badly shaken when Paul falls asleep at the wheel, and loses an arm in the resulting accident. This rather side-lines him during the rest of the film, which sees Lana (Ida Lupino), the wife of haulage magnate Ed Carlsen (Alan Hale), making a serious play for brother Joe, even though he's quite happily hitched to Cassie Hartley (Ann Sheridan). To relieve him of any doubts he might be having about *her* intentions, Lana simply murders her hubby, and then offers Joe a share of the business she inherits from him. When Joe continues to give her nothing more than the cold shoulder, she goes completely nuts, confesses to the murder and leaves Joe and Cassie rejoicing in their fidelity.

106

The acting in THEY DRIVE BY NIGHT is uniformly excellent, especially Lupino's rendition of the bitched-out road hussy, which gives Regina Baff (ROAD MOVIE) and Ann Savage (DETOUR) a run for their money. Bogart could have filled out his role better if he hadn't suffered an amputation, but maybe Walsh was saving him for HIGH SIERRA!

Considering his track record, it's interesting that Walsh chose a screenplay that contains none of the usual western/road movie analogies. But the director had few peers in his day, and was a master of entertaining melodrama who borrowed from no-one. At one point in THEY DRIVE BY NIGHT, George Raft bluntly states, "We're tougher than any truck that ever comes off the assembly line." Walsh could claim the same for his film.

USA   1940   93 mins.
Dir: Raoul Walsh   *Prod:* Mark Hellinger
Prod. Co: Warner Bros   *Script:* Jerry Wald and Richard Macaulay
Cast incl: George Raft, Humphrey Bogart, Ida Lupino, Ann Sheridan,
Gale Page, Alan Hale and Roscoe Karns

THUNDER ALLEY

Stockcar racing drama, and when I say stock, I mean it in the utilitarian sense, too. THUNDER ALLEY is a tawdry affair, memorable only for the sight of Annette Funicello, drunk out of her mind, driving around a deserted race track and running over Fabian's brother. Fabian's role is, guess what, the embittered racing driver and Annette is his bottle-hitting paramour (so *that's* what happens when a Mouseketeer gets too old to squeak). Slightly better executed than its generic peer, THE WILD RACERS, but there's not much in it... proof positive, in fact, that pop singers can't act and shouldn't try.

USA   1967   82 mins.
Dir: Richard Rush   *Prod:* Burt Topper
Prod. Co: Anglo Amalgamated   *Script:* n/a
Cast incl: Fabian, Annette Funicello, Jan Murray, Warren Berlinger,
Diane McBain, Stanley Adams and Mike Bell

Roger Corman never misses a trick, of course, so here is his version of the bootleg running movie. And in terms of action sequences, it must be said that THUNDER AND LIGHTNING has everything you'll find in WHITE LIGHTNING, THUNDER ROAD and even LAST AMERICAN HERO, but the price you pay is a trite script (by someone with the unlikely name of William Hjortsberg – another Corman joke?), and an imbalanced action: dialogue ratio which definitely favours the motors. CHARLIE'S ANGEL Kate Jackson doesn't have much of a chance to extend herself in the role of a frothy young actress (!) whose father, played by Roger Carmel, is David Carradine's main rival in the hooch hauling business. Carradine does his usual workmanlike job of playing a rather epicene miscreant, but THUNDER AND LIGHTNING is little more than another excuse for Corman and his protegees to smash up cars, people and buildings. Nothing else gets a look in.

USA   1977   93 mins.
Dir: Corey Allen   *Prod:* Roger Corman
Prod. Co: New World   *Script:* William Hjortsberg
Cast incl: David Carradine, Kate Jackson, Roger C. Carmel, Sterling Holloway, Ed Barth and Ron Feinberg

Property of National Screen Service Corporation. Licensed for use only in connection with the exhibition of this picture at the theatre licensing this material. Licensee agrees not to trade, sell or give it away, or permit others to use it, nor shall licensee be entitled to any credit upon return of this material. This material either must be returned or destroyed immediately after use.

1

THUNDER AND LIGHTNING
Released by 20th Century-Fox
Color by Deluxe®

COPYRIGHT © 1977 TWENTIETH CENTURY-FOX FILM CORPORATION

77/113

LITHO. IN U.S.A.

THUNDERBOLT AND LIGHTFOOT

In THUNDERBOLT AND LIGHTFOOT – one of his occasional comedy-thrillers – Clint Eastwood plays John 'Thunderbolt' Doherty, a bank robber out to recover the proceeds of a heist from his accomplices Red Leary (George Kennedy) and Goody

(Geoffrey Lewis). The trouble is that Leary and Goody think that *he's* the one who's absconded with the loot, and when they find him hiding out as a country preacher, his hide is only saved by the sudden intrusion of Lightfoot (Jeff Bridges), a young, itinerant car thief. Despite a carefree, quixotic attitude which offends his professionalism, Doherty doesn't have much choice but to run off with Lightfoot, and his misgivings soon turn in to a sort of begrudging friendship. Together they set off to find the Montana schoolhouse where Doherty believes the fourth member of the gang, now apparently dead, bricked up the money behind the blackboard. When they reach the supposed location, they're dismayed to find a modern college has been built on the site of the original school. Whilst cursing their luck, Goody and Leary turn up, and after a frantic car chase, Leary loses a clumsy fist-fight with Doherty who eventually convinces him he hasn't got the money. Lightfoot casually suggests that they start all over again and recreate the raid on the Montana Armoury vault which provided the original spoils. After arguing about it for a while, the others glumly concede to Lightfoot's suggestion. Finding local jobs to support themselves during the planning stage, they succeed in an audacious raid which features Lightfoot dressing up in drag to divert the sex-starved security guard, and the use of a 20mm cannon to penetrate the safe door. Goody, however, is wounded during their escape, and subsequently dumped by Leary when the police interrupt their progress. Leary then takes the money, badly brutalises Lightfoot, and runs off on his own. Dejectedly lamming it out of Montana, Doherty and the partly incapacitated Lightfoot accidently pass the old schoolhouse which has been transported and restored as an historical monument. To their delight, they remove the blackboard and find the money still sitting there. After buying the brand new Cadillac he's always yearned for, Lightfoot suddenly dies in its front seat, Leary's beating finally taking its toll.

Written and directed with definite traces of John Milius all over the place (the two co-wrote MAGNUM FORCE together), Michael Cimino nevertheless excels with his first solo feature. Although the story loses some momentum during its middle section as the four hoods prepare for the break-in, the pace is beautifully maintained elsewhere with the tough action sequences and the wry, villainish fraternity balancing each other like a pendulum. Moments of gloom or impasse dive engagingly into farce: the hick who rescues Doherty and Lightfoot on a deserted road and takes them on a crazed, switchback ride in his hopped-up Dodge then stops, unloads a truck full of white rabbits and starts shooting them. Or the sight of Goody and Leary, their big city thuggery deflated in a miasma of sweaty humiliation as they deliver ice-cream aboard a tiny tricycle. Although clearly contrived, these little vignettes fit naturally into the already screwed-up lives of these four, footling hoods, whose main frustration is in fact their mutual dependency.

The exposition of THUNDERBOLT AND LIGHTFOOT is largely based on Lightfoot's unwitting role as a catalyst, and Bridges delivers as bravura a performance as he did in THE LAST AMERICAN HERO. He plays Lightfoot as a cross between Charlie Chaplin and Elmer Gantry, a reckless, effervescent optimism tempered by a maverick cunning that he hasn't quite yet got a rein on. Doherty is his hero, his first big-time criminal acquaintance, and Clint Eastwood does a nice job of maintaining this crumbling facade, whilst clearly flattered by his partner's admiration. The irascible, sadistic Leary is played with maniacal gusto by one of my favourite character actors, George Kennedy, but Geoffrey Lewis as the weaker, slightly feminine Goody, underplays a role he doesn't seem exactly sure of.

THUNDERBOLT AND LIGHTFOOT has an underlying confidence which belies its pretensions as yet another Eastwood blockbuster. Its main strength is in its comic suspense, which is cleverly built around the basic gambits of a road movie. And in this latter respect we must again applaud Gary Loftin for some stylish driving sequences. Funnily enough, Cimino ends his film with a reference to another Loftin-stunted pic, VANISHING POINT. Both films have a song called 'Where Do We Go From Here?' playing over their credits – different songs, same gauche overstatement!

USA   1974   115 mins.
Dir: Michael Cimino   *Prod:* Robert Daley
Prod. Co: Malpaso   *Script:* Cimino
Cast incl: Clint Eastwood, Jeff Bridges, George Kennedy, Geoffrey
        Lewis, Catherine Bach, Gary Busey, Jack Dodson, Roy Jenson
        and Bill McKinney

THUNDER ROAD

Turned out by Robert Mitchum's own production company in 1958, THUNDER ROAD was a prime example of the sort of macho, men's movie that the star was happiest with.

From his own original story, James Philips wrote a rather average screenplay about moonshining and racketeering whose main virtue is the frequency with which Mr. Mitchum is called upon to punch his adversaries in the mouth. There's plenty of auto action, too, for Mitchum plays a man responsible for transporting the illegal hooch. The other main characters are dealt with by his real-life younger brother, Jim, who gets Bob's girlfriend (Sandra Knight) after he buys it in a big way behind the wheel. Is this incest, we ask ourselves?

Arthur Ripley's direction is uneven, and guest star Keely Smith doesn't need to sing, or indeed act, to embellish the proceedings.

USA   1940   94 mins.
Dir: Arthur Ripley   *Prod:* Robert Mitchum
Prod. Co: DRM Prods.   *Script:* James A. Philips
Cast incl: Mitchum, Jim Mitchum, Sandra Knight, Gene Barry, Trevor
        Bardette, Keely Smith, Betsy Holt and Jaques Aubuchon

TRUCK BUSTERS

Scraping the bottom of the oil drum as far as haulage biz movies are concerned, this flatulent meller is yet another rendering of the majors vs. independents parable. There's the usual violence and some exaggerated action footage, but it featured no-one of any real merit, before or after its release.

USA   1943   53 mins.
Dir: B. Reaves Eason   *Prod:* n/a
Prod. Co: Warner Bros.   *Script:* Robert Kent and Raymond Schrock
Cast incl: Richard Travis, Virginia Christine, Charles Lang, Ruth Ford,
        Richard Fraser and Frank Wilcox

TRUCK STOP WOMEN

Although due to an over-emphasis on naked female flesh, TRUCK STOP
WOMEN only seems to surface on the soft-porn circuit, Mark L. Lester's film is actually
an often riotous, if darkly cynical drama of trucking and criminal bravado.

Lieux Dressler plays Anna, the madame in the brothel she operates out of a
freeway truckstop, her daughter, Rose (Claudia Jennings) the star turn. John Martino is
Smith, an abrasive Mafiosa who tries to muscle in on Anna's lucrative business,
provoking an intensive war of attrition. There are some graphically exquisite scenes of
life on the road, including well observed rivalry between car and truck drivers, and a
lot of ketchup-embellished violence. The twisted relationship between Rose and Anna
is given a useful amount of attention, too. But no-one is ready for the scene when
daughter shoots mother in the back, and then promptly gets a bullet herself from the
sheriff (who's been deterred from clamping down on Rose's whorehouse primarily
because he's got a free tab there!).

TRUCK STOP WOMEN is an interesting and certainly enjoyable effort made
on the back of Lester's ultra-low budget STEEL ARENA, but a hundred times more
slickly.

USA   1974   82 mins.
Dir: Mark L. Lester   *Prod:* Lester
Prod. Co: LT Films   *Script:* Paul Deason and Lester
Cast incl: Lieux Dressler, Claudia Jennings, John Martino, Gene Drew,
        Dennis Fimple, Paul Carr, Eric Nord and Jennifer Burton

TWO LANE BLACKTOP

Director Monte Hellman is quoted as saying that he approaches all his films as comedies. He also said, prior to beginning work on TWO LANE BLACKTOP, that "I don't really know what my film is going to be about before I make it. I think I have a pretty good idea, but I'm willing to be surprised." Yet such statements conflict with the reality of the film that he eventually created: TWO LANE BLACKTOP is hardly a comedy, its rare moments of humour are largely incidental or metaphorical, and Hellman's control over the production is obvious and consummate.

Taking a Rudolph Wurlitzer/Will Cory script (written from Cory's own story) about itinerant, semi-professional drag racers, Hellman builds a movie of considerable subtlety, one that endeavours to define the spiritual ambivalence of a nation drifting in post-flower power social contradictions. Hardly comedy, heavy stuff in fact, and Hellman is working against significant odds by using a largely amateur cast.

The film opens with the Driver (James Taylor) and the Mechanic (Dennis Wilson) driving their primer-grey '57 Chevvy through the South West, looking for punters willing to back their cars against the barely disguised street dragster. A young woman (Laurie Bird) slips into the car whilst they're eating in a diner, but they ignore her when they return, and exchange few words during the rest of the day's drive. The Driver – each character is known only by his function – seems to think that the Girl is attracted to him, but has trouble showing any response. When he returns to the motel later that night, he hears her making love to the Mechanic, and sits dejectedly outside until they finish. The next day, they meet the bumptious owner of a brand new Pontiac GTO (Warren Oates), and accept his somewhat hesitant challenge to race to Washington, with ownership of the loser's car as the prize. A little later, GTO is already suffering engine trouble, and the Mechanic generously stops and offers to fix it. Whilst they're waiting for a nearby garage to open, the Girl wanders off, followed by GTO who rather touchingly tries to bridge a two generation age gap, and make-out with her. Meanwhile, the Mechanic finishes the repairs and drives off with the Girl and the Driver whilst GTO naps in his car. He eventually wakes and catches up with them, just in time to act as their unofficial manager and accept a bet on their behalf. The race is for serious money and although they're uneasy about GTO acting for them when he's also racing against them, they win this exciting, night-time challenge. GTO further irritates them, however, by taking off with the Girl. They are spurred into a bout of furious driving, finally spotting the Pontiac parked at yet another diner. As the three men bluntly argue the toss about who's chauffeuring the Girl, the first time any of them have made their feelings clear about her, she is seen ironically through the diner's window, climbing onto the back of a motorcycle. The two parties react to this in different ways. GTO continues on his aimless odyssey, picking up hitch-hikers and boasting outlandishly of his unlikely exploits. The Chevvy boys are seen taking on one final, symbolic challenge, and as the Driver shuts the car door in readiness for the race, there's a hollow thud, like a vault closing. The soundtrack dims to an eerie hiss, the colour bleaches out of the film stock and the car lurches forward in slow motion, finally exploding as the celluloid flips out of the projector and burns in the carbon arc.

This ending is the most excessive example of the dreamy, often unreal quality that pervades TWO LANE BLACKTOP. Jack Deerson's photography is sparse, but Hellman consistently places some small activity or image in a corner or background, giving which distract the eye and gently distort the view. (This is a trick he developed in his two earlier westerns, THE SHOOTING and the brilliant, RIDE THE WHIRLWIND). The surreal mood augured by the photography and art direction is enhanced, perhaps by default, by the oblique and understated reactions of the main characters. They use few words and display few emotions, as if they've long since accepted that they are helpless victims of their fate: they go through the motions of the

Great American Journey, driven by some vague hope of finding a personal nirvana somewhere along the line, knowing that it's unlikely, but not really caring one way or the other. This nihilism is most strongly invested in the Girl, who casually drifts from one situation to another, and when she can't find room for her few pathetic belongings as she takes off with the motorcyclist, she simply dumps her shoulder bag in the parking lot.

To the Chevvy owners, freedom is slightly more tangible and attainable. They can win it, but we wonder what they would do with a whole bunch of prize-money that freedom represents? Buy another hot-rod? Their car is all that seems to matter to them, the Mechanic even refers to it in the female tense, and drag racing is all they know. The prospect of a *person* offering them something they haven't already got was flickering through their minds when they met the Girl, but neither of them could take the risk. To quote Peter Fonda in EASY RIDER, "They blew it."

GTO comes from a different caste than the others, one that watched with some envy as a generation took acid, created new and radical social rites and used their new-found affluence in ways hitherto considered irresponsible. GTO can't grasp that, but he tries. He tells everyone he won his car in a crap game, offers a choice of music and drugs to his hitch-hikers (he, himself prefers the bottle and MOR crooners), and clearly believes that driving around in his big, glitzy muscle car like this gives him a playboy persona. His unconvincing mien provides the only deliberate comedy in TWO LANE BLACKTOP, for example, when he tries to shrug off casually the advances of a young gay he picks up ("I ain't got time for that man, this is competition"), or when he tries to console the widow of a car crash victim, having just loud-mouthed her on the virtues of fast driving ("Must've been a city car killed him," he mutters).

Like the others, GTO is looking for the impossible and knows it, but his is a more complex characterisation and one Warren Oates carries off with exactly the right degree of self-deception. But then Oates is the only professional in any of the main roles, which accounts in part for the inert delivery of the other performances. This clearly worried Hellman before he started the film, but it's equally obvious that he rigorously tutored Bird, Wilson and Taylor in their handling of lines. (Taylor later

attested that Hellman was indeed "a control freak" during the making of TWO LANE BLACKTOP). Hellman compensates for their lack of expression by slowly dropping hints and signs that slowly fit together into a character, a process which contrasts with lives which revolve around fast cars and fast action. Paradoxically, though, there's enough material in Hellman's movie to satisfy anyone not even remotely interested in cars. But if they *are* auto aficionados, BLACKTOP is a joy, for Hellman and technical adviser Jay Wheatley have gone to some pains to authenticate the vehicles in the movie, and ensure that the driving and the racing accurately and lovingly reflect its folksy source.

All in all, a fascinating film and one that's damn near impossible to dislike.

USA   1971   101 mins.
Dir: Monte Hellman   *Prod:* Michael S. Laughlin
Prod. Co: Universal/Laughlin Ents.   *Script:* Rudolph Wurlitzer and
                                         Will Cory
Photog: Jack Deerson
Cast incl: The Driver – James Taylor; The Mechanic – Dennis Wilson;
        GTO – Warren Oates; The Girl – Laurie Bird; also featuring:
        David Drake, Richard Ruth, Jaclyn Hellman, Bill Keller, W.H.
        Harrison and Tom Green

THE VAN

Unleashed on an unsuspecting, and largely unimpressed world by the same team that gave us THE POM POM GIRLS, THE VAN is a dumb story about a young jerk who, like most Californians, believes that his dream vehicle, in this case a gaudily customised van, will get him lots of chick action. It doesn't, thank heavens, but even that faint parable is lost amongst a welter of male chauvinism, poor scripting and awful photography. Miss it.

USA   1977   90 mins.
Dir: Sam Grossman   *Prod:* Paul Lewis
Prod. Co: Crown International   *Script:* Celia Susan Cotelo and
                                         Rob Rosenthal
Cast incl: Stuart Getz, Deborah White, Michael Lloyd, Harry Moses,
        Stephen Oliver, Connie Lisa Marie and Danny Devito

VANISHING POINT

Elsewhere in the book I have used VANISHING POINT as a yardstick and made feckless allusions to its excellence, something which I am now happy to justify. But first, the story.

Arriving in Denver with a car he's ferried from San Francisco, Kowalski (Barry Newman) tells his receiving agent that he wants to return to California immediately. Following some argument, he's reluctantly given a supercharged Dodge Charger and, after collecting amphetemines and an impossible wager that he won't make it back to San Francisco by three the following afternoon, he zooms off. Breaking the speed limits and the police road blocks set up to apprehend him for doing so, it's established that Kowalski is a troubled man, driven as much as actually driving. But by what? A blind black dee-jay, Super Soul (Cleavon Little), hears of Kowalski's misdeeds over the police radio-band, decides that he symbolises "the last free man on earth" and deifies him throughout his high pressure radio show. Incidents abound en route: attempted abduction by two honeymooning homosexuals; a fiercesome duel with a crazy Jaguar driver; an old, impoverished prospector who takes Kowalski to meet a raggedy religous sect; a lone Hell's Angel and his girlfriend who help him avoid a road-block... all of this punctuated by Super Soul's cryptic advice about the cops' activities. The police are not, however, happy about the dee-jay's efforts to ease Kowalski's flight. Their response is to send plainclothesmen to his radio station, beat him up, and force him to broadcast false information designed to lead Kowalski into a trap. Despite this, he manages to get to the Nevada border but, within reach of his "freedom", he faces an impenetrable barrier of earth moving machinery, which we'd seen being positioned at the start of the film. (Throughout the chase, there have also been brief flashbacks of Kowalski suffering as an incorruptible cop, a motorcycle racer in a career-ending crash, a lover who loses his girl in a drowning accident.)

Although director Richard Sarafian readily admitted to me that VANISHING POINT bears clear references to EASY RIDER's wishful, wistful quest for America, it is a film that excels on several other levels. Essential to Sarafian and screenwriter Guillermo Cain's view of America is that it will be seen by a commercial cinema audience, and so VANISHING POINT has little of the hip jargon and affectation that now dates RIDER (and alienated many of those who originally saw it). Further accepting the parameters of the mainstream marketplace, Sarafian invested his film with the sort of action and easily assimilated moral observations that are the hallmarks of exploitation movies.

VANISHING POINT is well endowed with the cut and thrust of the chase, and the character and motives of its hero are clearly stated by the flashbacks. Here is a man with two failed careers and one broken heart; flash-flash-flash-*boom*, we know who he is. The strength of his resolve is something that develops more subtly as we watch him react to the problems and possibilities he confronts on his trip. The audience can take or leave them, however, because there's a serious, well maintained car chase going on and, unlike movies like SUGARLAND EXPRESS or TWO LANE BLACKTOP, it is this that deliberately dominates the storyline.

Credit for this must go to Cary Loftin for the unwavering, infectious grip of Kowalski's actual driving manners, and Sarafian's understanding of the dynamics of fast, long distance road work. It is appropriate that Kowalski is delivering a Charger, for this monstrous 6-litre machine was the apogee of the over-the-top muscle car, perfect for gonzo driving tactics. John Alonzo's camera puts this in a nice perspective, frequently distancing itself from the car, watching it move slowly across the countryside like an ant on a window-ledge and then, wham, edits into the snarling interior where Kowalski is pitting himself against the torque of the gears and the inertia of the steering wheel. The emphasis is on both the power and the vulnerability of the automobile – Kowalski being caught between the lure of losing himself to the sanctuary of that great landscape, or wedding his fate to the steel and rubber that he's so familiar with. But time is running out for him as the police close in, and his adventures along the way take on a more urgent, even desperate quality towards the film's end.

There's symbolism there if you want it, of course. The gay couple who try to rip Kowalski off, represent the darker side of sexual tolerance, although Sarafian handles it with great humour – their broken down old car strewn with "Just Married" slogans and paraphernalia. The old timer, reduced to trapping rattlesnakes which he sells to the boorish cult leader, can be seen as a paradox between new and old human values. And the Hell's Angel who helps him escape is a rather arch development of that same theme; philanthropy still exists, although not where you would expect to find it. There is also the business of Super Soul, black *and* blind, but hip to Kowalski, who he sees as the avatar of some spiritual crusade. But Kowalski, and indeed the audience if it likes, can do without any of this often pretentious allegory: "Go to hell," he grunts at Super Soul's radio aggrandisement at one point.

Rare is the chase movie that isn't beset by heavy metaphor, and VANISHING POINT perhaps has more than its fair share, especially when the point is harshly laboured by the soundtrack music. Like EASY RIDER and BADLANDS, Sarafian accompanies many of the driving sequences with contemporary pop music, much of it directly or implicitly religious and most of it below par: 'Dear Jesus God' by Segarini and Bishop (who?), 'You've Got To Believe', which is actually performed in the movie during a quasi-revivalist meeting, by Delaney & Bonnie & Friends, 'Sweet Jesus', by Red Teagel (who?) and 'Sing Out For Jesus' by Kim Carnes. So does Sarafian see conventional Christianity as an antidote to the prejudice and hypocrisy offered in his and EASY RIDER's vision of America?

"Well not exactly," claims the director. "It kind of worked out that way. I originally had Sid Kaiser and Alan Pariso write a whole score, based on an improvisation by Delaney & Bonnie and with Rita Coolidge, Big Mama Thornton and Leon Russell performing it. And it was terrific. But Lionel Newman, who was head of Music at Fox, said he wouldn't allow us to use anybody who Fox didn't have the publishing on. So I said, 'What about getting your nephew, Randy Newman, involved?'. And he said, 'Nah, he's not any good'! What happened in the end was that we got about fifty young musicians and showed them the film, and they all went off and came back with some songs out of which we picked the most suitable." Putting the onus for the religious content with a bunch of composers doesn't really answer the question, though. So I asked Sarafian, a portly, avuncular man in his early forties, what exactly the spiritual message of the film was.

"Well the story was originally about an older man – I wanted George C. Scott for the part but the studio insisted on Newman – who meets this young lady, falls in love, and is kind of opened up by her and introduced to speed in a whole 'nother dimension. But then she dies and he's left alone, but unable to return to the lifestyle he led before he met her. So he's kind of lost, and kind of desperate. The thing about the film that upset me most was that the point of the story had been changed... I had a better ending. The thing was that Kowalski drives towards the bulldozers and he sees a gap between them, and he goes for it, and he *makes* it. And the Super Soul, who's been sensing Kowalski's feelings throughout this thing, goes 'YEAH!', instead of grieving – which is his reaction in the version you saw. It was a more upbeat ending, but that wasn't the point. The point was that Kowalski saw that gap as his 'vanishing point', where he takes off onto some other plane, lets his spirit leave his body, goes off into some other world... whatever. The script called for him to commit suicide by hitting those 'dozers, and I wanted Super Soul's reaction to *that* to be upbeat, because he could sense that Kowalski was finally being released. But Zanuck (Richard Zanuck, boss of 20th Century Fox at the time) wouldn't allow that, he thought it was too esoteric. And he wouldn't allow the ending where Kowalski gets through, either.

"Which was odd, because Zanuck really liked another scene I shot, which was cut by the studio after Zanuck had been fired: Kowalski picks up this strange woman hitch-hiker, Charlotte Rampling, all dressed in black with a huge black hat. He makes love to her, and takes off her hat, and she's *bald*. The next morning he wakes up and she's gone... she was a premonition of course, a symbol of death, and at that moment there's an acceptance of his fate, of his 'vanishing point', which made a lot more sense of the ending."

Despite cuts and the lost message of its ending, VANISHING POINT is a masterpiece. It has pace, style and enough thoughtful comment lying beneath its unashamedly commercial gloss to satisfy any cineaste and every car freak. VANISHING POINT is arguably Richard Sarafian's best film to date, although he is probably better known for MAN IN THE WILDERNESS and RUN WILD RUN FREE.

Great Britain	1971	107 mins

Dir: Richard Sarafian   *Prod:* Norman Spencer
Prod. Co: Cupid Prod.   *Script:* Guillermo Cain
Photog: John A. Alonzo   *Stunt Dir:* Cary Loftin
Cast incl: Kowalski – Barry Newman; Super Soul – Cleavon Little; Prospector – Dean Jagger; Vera – Victoria Medlin; Hell's Angel – Timothy Scott; also featuring: Paul Koslo, Bob Donner, Anthony James, Arthur Malet, Severn Darden, Delaney & Bonnie & Friends and Gilda Texter

WAGES OF FEAR

If ROAD MOVIE offers the ultimate in trucking realism, WAGES OF FEAR tops it in its ability to focus on the tactile dangers of driving big, heavy vehicles, using them as a basis for nerve-wracking suspense. And that's only the half of it, for the film is also a finely drawn human drama, the story of four disconsolate has-beens who have ended up trapped in a slime-pit of a remote, Central American oil town.

The group starts out as a trio; Mario (Yves Montand), a young Corsican, Luigi (Folco Lulli), a chipper Italian and Bimba (Peter Van Eyck), a reticent German,

117

but they are joined by Jo (Charles Vanel), an ageing French hood on the run. They quarrel, they drink, they have thinly disguised homosexual liaisons and are clearly desperate to find an escape route back to a world where they can recover their dignity. When Jo arrives, with his fading Parisian charm and criminal mystique, he attracts Mario away from the maternal Luigi, provoking a tension in the group which subsequently heightens the excitement of the journey. (This element of the film, plus a suggestion of American political and financial exploitation of third world countries, was thought inappropriate for that nation's cinema audiences. The version of WAGES OF FEAR shown in the U.S.A. was therefore cut by some 34 minutes, rendering much of its early sequences confused and apparently irrelevant).

A cargo of nitroglycerene is urgently required to blow out an oil fire 300 miles away, and the four men jump at the opportunity to drive the two trucks that are to deliver it. Despite the treacherous roads and tracks involved in the journey, and the knowledge that the oil company are sending twice the amount of highly volatile explosive needed – because they anticipate only one of the trucks will make it through – the men are willing to take the risk. The reward is $2000 dollars apiece, and the "wages of fear" are freedom. The devices director Henri Clouzot uses to keep us gnawing at our finger-nails were not new, even in 1953, but he squeezes every ounce of suspense out of them: The trucks are forced to reverse out on to a shakey wooden trestle hanging over a precipice; a huge boulder lying in their path has to be

detonated; Luigi and Bimba's truck blows up and leaves a huge pool of oil which the remaining vehicle has to somehow get through. In this real hair-raiser of a scene, Jo wades into the oil to guide Mario through, loses his footing and is crushed to death under the wheels. Mario's concern, of course, is primarily with getting the money, which he eventually does. He also buys it in a big way when he crashes on the return journey.

Clouzot's style is perhaps a little too mannered and grandiose, but he certainly pulls no punches and even when handling the subtleties of the men's relationship, he effectively conveys the frustration and violence born out of their despair. The men are selfish, cold and elicit our sympathies only because it's implied

that they'll become better human beings once liberated from their jungle prison.
Maybe.

Elsewhere you can read of William Friedkin's ineffectual remake of WAGES
OF FEAR, curiously titled THE SORCERER. Despite the financial and technical
resources at his command, Friedkin's film is vastly inferior to the original.

France/Italy   1953   140 mins
Dir: Henri G. Clouzot
Prod. Co: Filmsonor/Vera Film   *Script:* Clouzot
Cast incl: Yves Montand, Charles Vanel, Folco Lulli, Peter Van Eyck,
                   Vera Clouzot, William Tubbs and Centa

WEEKEND

A sitting duck for film semiotics, Jean-Luc Godard's WEEKEND has
constantly attracted weighty philosophical, political and structural analysis, little of
which you're going to get from me. Followers of the French cinema will know pretty
much what to expect from the movie anyway... road movie converts with no interest in
the finer points of *nouvelle vague* will simply have their breath taken away.

WEEKEND doesn't really have a plot, although in its early minutes there are
threads of a murder conspiracy, betrayals and sexual motifs, all soon forgotten as the
central couple, played by Jean Yanne and Mireille Darc, join the Friday exodus from
Paris that provides the film's title. In a daringly long take, we pass a traffic jam, a
thrombosis of burnt, broken-down and crashed vehicles, mangled bodies, ball-
playing children, blaring klaxons, smoke and screaming. A metaphor for life, or a
metaphor for the life that the automobile has made for us? Who knows *or* cares, the
sensual barrage has only just begun; cars are stolen, gas stations searched out, and we
are gradually made aware that the couple have been literally driven mad. But their
crazed desperation with everything behind and around them is not empty, or numbed
into a state of suspended animation as it is in KINGS OF THE ROAD, or RADIO ON, its
most obvious reference points. Instead Godard's script and direction, or rather his
concept, calls for a kind of angry ebullience, packed with cartoon paradox and visual
anachronism; a Mozart sonata, a love song sung in a telephone booth, battles with
spray paint and tennis balls, long diatribes on the plight of the African tribes, bloody
accidents and, ultimately, cannibalism.

To further confuse his intentions, Godard flavours his collage of a world gone out of control with some little semantic jokes. Cards flash up between edits: "FAUX..." followed by "TOGRAPHIE", "ANAL...YSE".

In fact, despite its anarchic allusions and doomstruck pessimism, WEEKEND is a comedy in the true sense of the term, but one calculated to leave you disturbed rather than feeling warmly and generously entertained. Whatever Godard's true inspiration and intentions, it is an ambitious, enormously startling enterprise defying rational description, much less critical resolution, and needs to be seen at least twice to be fully savoured.

France/Italy   1968   103 mins
Dir: Jean-Luc Godard
Prod. Co: Comacico/Copernic Lira (France),   *Script:* Godard
      Ascot Cineraid (Italy)
Cast incl: Jean Yanne, Mireille Darc, Jean-Pierre-Kaflon, Valerie Langrange, Jean-Pierre Leaud, Paul Gegauff and Yves Alfonso

WHITE LIGHTNING

Introducing us to convicted moonshiner, Gator Muklusky (Burt Reynolds), who somehow staggered on to feature in a sequel titled with his forename, WHITE LIGHTNING is an inoffensive little story about revenge. The object of Gator's angst is a corrupt sheriff, played by Ned Beatty, who is the under FBI investigation over his alleged involvement in the illicit whisky trade. Gator is released from jail to help nail the sheriff, his resolve hardened by the lawman's complicity in his younger brother's murder.

Scripted by B.W.L. Norton (CONVOY, OUTLAW BLUES), the film is basically a vehicle for Mr. Reynolds to flutter a few female hearts and wreck a few cars. Although the Arthur Gardner/Jules Levy production is capable in every respect, WHITE LIGHTNING comes off a poor second to THE LAST AMERICAN HERO due to lightweight, stereotypical characterisations and its depiction of the bootleg trade as something out of Marvel comics.

USA   1973   101 mins
Dir: Joseph Sargent   *Prod:* Arthur Gardner and Jules Levy
Prod. Co: United Artists   *Script:* B.W.L Norton
Cast incl: Burt Reynolds, Jennifer Billingsley, Ned Beatty, Matt Clark, Louise Latham, Diana Ladd, R.G. Armstrong and Conlan Carter

WHITE LINE FEVER

Jonathan Kaplan's first film was an out-of-the-blue directing job for Roger Corman, NIGHT CALL NURSES ("Frontal nudity from the waist up, total nudity from behind and no pubic hair. Now Go To Work."). A series of low-rent exploiters followed before he got a chance to call the shots with WHITE LINE FEVER.

The story concerns Air Force vet. Carrol Jo Hummer (Jan-Michael Vincent) who takes out a loan to buy a truck and marry his sweetheart, Jerri (Kay Lenz). In trying to find haulage work, he discovers that the industry is run by Mafia-style racketeers who regularly deal in contraband goods. Virtuous to a fault (the Air Force training, see), he refuses to get involved with such business, and receives a beating from thugs working for Haller (Slim Pickens), the boss of one of these outfits. He then holds Haller at gunpoint in order to get a load, which Carrol delivers with the help of token negro, Pops Dinwiddie (Sam Laws). His courageous stance wins him the support of other small, hitherto timorous truckers, and more work from Haller, but after he's given a cargo of rotton fruit for a long haul and then loudly threatens Haller, a conspiracy between the racketeers and the public prosecutor puts Carrol on a murder charge. Needless to say, Carrol finally beats the forces of evil and receives sainthood amongst the down-trodden trucking community.

This WALKING TALL-type saga is confidently executed by Kaplan and a well chosen cast of faces old and new. Although Hummer's early recourse to violence is justified in the screenplay as a means to a noble end, it's one he makes too often, and too zealously to sit well with an audience. (Shades of Kaplan's previous Corman blood-bath, TRUCK TURNER). The inarticulately grateful small-timers, the wife who conceals her pregnancy in fear of exacerbating Hummer's already terrible plight, the thug who sets fire to their home... all these plottings pile on the melodrama perhaps a little too heavily. But when all is said and done, WHITE LINE FEVER is a valiant effort by a young director to shake off the fetters of exploitation. And Cary Loftin drives, crashes and ballet-dances the trucks!

USA	1975	89 mins

Dir: Jonathan Kaplan   *Prod:* John Kemeny
Prod. Co: White Line Fever Syndicate   *Script:* Ken Friedman and Kaplan
Cast incl: Jan-Michael Vincent, Kay Lenz, Slim Pickens, Sam Laws, R.G. Armstrong, Don Porter, Ron Nix and Leigh French

THE WILD ANGELS

This is the film that launched the whole outlaw gang syndrome, notwithstanding THE WILD ONE, bringing several hitherto unknown names into the limelight they would later flourish under (or behind). Produced and directed under Roger Corman himself, THE WILD ANGELS has Peter Bogdanovitch as its assistant director, Monte Hellman as editor, Richard Moore in charge of the camera and Charles Griffith providing the script. The cast featured Peter Fonda in the first of his many B-road movies, Nancy Sinatra, Bruce Dern and Michael J. Pollard as members of a California bike gang.

WILD ANGELS is simply a stylised chronicle of a few days in the angels' hum-drum round of a-rapin' an a-fightin'. Such plot as there is revolves around the death of one of their number, seriously injured – along with a cop – during a fracas with a rival gang. Fearful of what might happen to him in hospital, Fonda & Co. remove him to their H.Q. where he snuffs it. A bent undertaker is bribed to lay out the corpse in a backwater church and, after the preacher has been tied up and the church trashed, the gang hoist their stiffened chum out of his coffin and prop him up with a cigarette in his mouth, so's he can "watch" the orgy they embark on. A motley cortege of bikers transport the body to a cemetery after the bash (where do they get their energy from, these kids?), which prompts a bloody battle between the gang and the local township. As police sirens rent the air, most of the gang run off but Fonda, muttering that "there's no place else to go", stays behind to face justice.

Fonda's half-hearted contrition at the movie's end was an effective sop to the howl of indignation that rose up throughout America following THE WILD ANGELS' release. Such protest also gathered the loud approval of many normally tolerant film critics when the film was selected as the *official* American entry for the prestigious Venice Film Festival in 1966. In addition to its sacrilegious pretensions, ANGELS also includes scenes of gang rape, a young negress being raped in hospital and endless drug and alcohol abuse – all activities that the youth of America routinely indulged in, of course. Corman's reaction to such moral panic was, predictably enough, to claim that his film did little more than dramatise reality, albeit a small and secular one. He told 'Saturday Night Review' in September 1966, that "Little shown on the screen had not occurred in reality; he had used actual 'leather boys', all in their mature twenties... and revealed that the gang members portrayed were all on the low side in intelligence, that not a few were homosexually inclined, that they had failed to find a place for themselves in 'square society', and behaved as they did for psychopathic reasons, as well as because of parental and social neglect. He hoped audiences would be able to discern for themselves these motivations, but may have missed a beat here and there."

Later on, Corman adopted a slightly more metaphysical view when interviewed by 'Film Comment' in Autumn 1971: "I see man to a certain extent as being adrift in a partially hostile, partially indifferent universe, and I see a struggle there. In some of (my) fantasy films, I see an optimistic outlook for man's attempts to come to grips with – call it a human situation. In realistic films, I see a pessimistic outlook."

Roger Corman earnestly discussing "man's attempts to come to grips with a human situation" never stopped him from vulgarising its worst excesses and selling them back to an eager audience. With THE WILD ANGELS, this is certainly the case and, depending on whether you saw the 93, 90 or 83 minute version, you were bombarded with every type of theatrical repellent in Corman's not inconsiderable bag of tricks. And yet by 1966, the director had still not perfected some of the techniques that gave his films at least a semblance of big studio professionalism (see introduction). The wobbly, hand-held camera panning rapidly through fight scenes may be an effective method of conveying the dynamics of the action, but it also exhibits an amateurishness which abets the cliches of the script in unwittingly promoting kitsch. This traditional Corman legacy is strongly evident in ANGELS, and although the film could be seen as morally execrable and in appalling taste, it would never be taken seriously if it had been released today. The acting alone is 100% implausible.

However, it was a young, urban audience who originally went to see THE WILD ANGELS in an era when Annette Funicello getting kissed was about as salacious as you could get on the silver screen. Fears for their moral welfare and a subsequent decline into the sort of behaviour the film evidently condoned were what concerned the establishment. Perhaps the most eloquent defence of that criticism came from Andrew Sarris:

"Many will complain that this sort of thing is irresponsible and even untrue. The newsreels of swastika bearing youths in Cicero are all too real, however, and nothing is to be gained from burying our heads in the sands of decorum. A frightful tension haunts our society. However, much as a movie like THE WILD ANGELS exploits this tension, it also exorcises the evil involved by simply acting it out."

USA   1966   93, 90 and 83 minute prints all in circulation
Dir: Roger Corman   *Prod:* Roger Corman
Prod. Co: American International   *Script:* Charles B. Griffith
Photog: Richard Moore   *Stunt Dir:* n/a
Cast incl: Heavenly Blues – Peter Fonda; Mike – Nancy Sinatra; Loser – Bruce Dern; Joint – Lou Procopio; Bull Puckey – Coby Denton; Frankenstein – Buck Taylor; also featuring: Norma Alden, Michael J. Pollard, Diane Ladd, Joan Shawlee, Gayle Hunnicutt, Art Baker and Frank Maxwell

THE WILD ONE

Apart from the startling opening shots, there's very little to do with motorcycling in THE WILD ONE, which is why it doesn't really warrant coverage in this book. It is also a notoriously well-known film, banned by the British censors for 14 years on account of unchecked violence that today seems tame by even the outlaw standards of the late 'sixties. THE WILD ONE is generally recognised as the precursor, albeit prematurely, of all those production line B-features, and it marked the start of Marlon Brando's badass enigma – for those reasons alone I can't deny it a mention.

Brando as the moody, mumbling gang leader who takes his boys on a rampage through a small country town, dominates the film. But Lee Marvin as a rival outlaw boss has a nice, shambling malevolence and Mary Murphy is a bundle of laughs as the apple-pie perfect sheriff's daughter. In fact the film is now camp rather than disturbing: big, bad Brando doesn't even kill anyone – his runaway motorcycle does. No wonder Harley-Davidsons became mandatory biker transport after THE WILD ONE!

USA   1953   79 mins
Dir: Laslo Benedek   *Prod:* Stanley Kramer
Prod. Co: Kramer/Columbia   *Script:* John Paxton
Cast incl: Marlon Brando, Lee Marvin, Mary Murphy, Robert Keith, Jay
              C. Flippen, Peggy Maley, Hugh Sanders, Ray Teal and John
              Brown

THE WILD RACERS

Some of the Corman alumnae associated with this drab little enterprise must have wished that it had more in common with his YOUNG RACERS than a similarity of title. Conceived, perhaps, as nothing more than a buoy for Fabian's flagging singing career, THE WILD RACERS is the old yawn of the fish-cold, ultra-dedicated motor racer who finally succumbs to the feminine wiles of the determined floosie. B-movie busy-body, Mimsy Farmer is the Ms. in question, and even her wiles aren't plausible, never mind her lines. The film relies instead on racing photography styled on that of GRAND PRIX, which conspicuously fails to make the grade. But that's hardly surprising on a budget that couldn't have been more than $50.

USA   1968   79 mins
Dir: Daniel Haller   *Prod:* Joel Rapp
Prod. Co: American Intl.   *Script:* Max House
Cast incl: Fabian, Mimsy Farmer, Judy Cornwall, David Landers,
              Warwick Sims and Alan Haufreci

WINNING

Lying somewhere between LE MANS and GRAND PRIX in its commitment to motor racing veracity, WINNING has a better storyline than either of them. Paul Newman is the mandatory race-ace who whisks a small-town Avis rent-a-car soubrette (Joanne Woodward, a/k/a Mrs. Newman) into his glamorous sphere of operations, and after proposing marriage to her, that means taking on her 16 year old son, too. But Woodward is soon relegated to the metaphorical pits by the demands of the job – and Newman's taste for partying. When Newman finds his once-too-often neglected wife in a motel room bed with his arch racing rival, played by Robert Wagner. he signals "finito". Although admitting guilt to himself, he can't expunge it in any other way but taking revenge on Wagner in the Indianapolis 500. But Woodward's son, Richard Thomas, isn't prepared to let Newman go that easily (he wants driving lessons, of course), and plays marriage guidance counsellor.

The relationship between the love-locked trio is believable and mercifully low on schmaltz, contrary to Newman's dealings with his racing buddies which are a bit too macho and bacchanalian to be true. WINNING is a longish film which allows time for the story to work itself through to its (predictable) conclusion without hamming it up in deference to the racing action. The latter is cleverly done, not quite as contrived as Saul Bass and John Frankenheimer's visual artifice in GRAND PRIX, but director James Goldstone draws on his t.v. experience, using fast edits and close-in camera pans to exude a contagious sensation of speed and the dynamics of the sport.

One of Newman's lesser films perhaps, but none the worse for that in its own right.

USA	1969	123 mins
Dir: James Goldstone		*Prod:* John Foreman
Prod. Co: Universal/Jennings Land		*Script:* Howard Rodman

Cast incl: Paul Newman, Joanne Woodward, Robert Wagner, Richard Thomas, David Sheiner and Clu Gulager

Roger Corman's first tilt at auto-movies, THE YOUNG RACERS flaunts the director's keep-it-moving-and-hang-the-storyline attitude to good effect.

It stars William Campbell as an embittered motor racing champ and Mark

A LITTLE DEATH EACH DAY...
A LOT OF LOVE EVERY NIGHT!
"THEY TREATED BEAUTIFUL WOMEN
AS IF THEY WERE FAST CARS...
...ROUGH!"

ACTUALLY
FILMED AT
THE GRAND PRIX
TRACKS OF THE WORLD!

THE YOUNG
RACERS

AN AMERICAN INTERNATIONAL PICTURE IN *PATHÉCOLOR*

STARRING
MARK DAMON · WILLIAM CAMPBELL · LUANA ANDERS AND FEATURING THE INTERNATIONAL PLAYGIRLS
ROGER CORMAN · R WRIGHT CAMPBELL · LES BAXTER

Damon, a writer whose fiancée defects to Campbell. This prompts Damon to trek round the European racing circus with his "secretary", Luana Anders, to gather dirt for a book exposing the man as a charlatan. Quite how a freelance hack can afford to take a secretary all over Europe with him is not made clear, neither is the identity of Campbell when he's actually racing (stock footage, I wonder?). But the camerawork is fairly solid and the general pace of the film meets all the Corman parameters. Assistant director Charles Griffith would probably have done better writing down to the drive-in market this pic was undoubtedly aimed at, but instead we have R. Wright Campbell coming out with incongruous prose seemingly held over from Corman's gothic horror films. Characters calling each other "Posturing dilletantes" and saying that they "don't want to be your inner ear", just don't cut it in an auto race drama of this or indeed any other ilk.

USA   1963   82 mins
Dir: Roger Corman   *Prod:* Roger Corman
Prod. Co: Alta Vista   *Script:* R. Wright Campbell
Cast incl: William Campbell, Mark Damon, Luana Anders, Patrick
             Magee, John McLaren, Maria Versini, Christina Gregg and
             Anthony Marsh

YOUR THREE MINUTES ARE UP

This uneven medium budget cine-odyssey is what might have happened had KINGS OF THE ROAD been done for laughs.

YOUR THREE MINUTES ARE UP stars Beau Bridges as Charlie, a rather timid 9-to-5'er dominated by his fiancee, Betty (Janet Margolin), and his philandering friend, Mike (Ron Leibman). The film opens as Mike is planning to leave town after his car's been repossessed and his social security withdrawn. He pursuades Charlie to drive him to the airport, but during the run out there, he talks him into going all the way up the coast highway to Santa Barbara. There follows a rapid sequence of confidence tricks, petty and otherwise, usually involving Charlie's gullability as a pivotal factor. Charlie's forced education in the criminal arts is complimented by Mike's attempts to turn him into a womaniser like himself. When Betty turns up and catches the two of them seducing a pair of girls in a motel room, Charlie angrily dismisses her in an apparent demonstration of his new-found maturity. However, after Mike tries to repeat an insurance scam they successfully carried out earlier, and then beats up a garage hand, Charlie decides he's had enough and tells Mike to hitch off on his own. The last shot shows Charlie crying in his car.

The rapport between the con-man and the hesitant novice is nicely essayed and often hilarious, but YOUR THREE MINUTES ARE UP, with its reliance on farce that becomes more and more puerile, and editing that gets more and more contrived, wearies its audience towards the end. So too do the personalities of the two main characters, both of whom are pushed to their initially engaging limits with virtually no relief from anyone else, all other parts being written in by James Dixon as brief butts or foils for the whacky antics of Mike and Charlie. Douglas Schwartz is too fond of his picaresque notions to consider the effects of their relentless pursuit, but YOUR THREE MINUTES is at least professionally whipped into action.

USA   1973   92 mins
Dir: Douglas Schwartz   *Prod:* Jerry Gershwin
Prod. Co: Minutes Company   *Script:* James Dixon
Cast incl: Beau Bridges, Ron Leibman, Janet Margolin, Kathleen
             Freeman, David Ketchum, Read Morgan and Stu Nisbet